TRANSMISSION
OF THE
FLAME

JEAN KLEIN

Edited by Emma Edwards

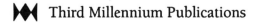 Third Millennium Publications

Library of Congress Catalog Card No.: 90-83516
ISBN No.: 1-877769-22-3

Cover Photograph by John Chase Lewis
Design and typography by Janet Andrews, Desktop Studio
Printed in the United States of America
First Printing: October 1990
Second Printing: August 1993

Acknowledgments

We give heartfelt thanks to Janet Andrews and Mary Dresser for the many hours they spent helping to prepare the text for printing and for their willingness to handle the myriad details related to publishing the book. Their unconditional support has been invaluable. Many thanks also to all those who transcribed the tapes that are the basis for this book, especially Pamela Lightbody and Don Wetherly in England, whose clear transcriptions made the going much easier. And, finally, deepest gratitude to Dennis Lewis and Warren Perrine for their generous donations, which made the publication of this book possible.

Preface

People often ask, "What are the talks like in Holland? Are the questions the same in France as in Italy? How do the dialogues in America differ from those in England? Are there differences in the types of questions asked in the different countries?" Here, then, is a book of dialogues recorded during seminars in four of the countries Jean Klein visits. As they all appear within a span of eleven months, one can see certain themes in the teaching carried through and approached a little differently each time.

Although the talks have been considerably edited to make the spoken word intelligible and consistent for the reader, they have been left as much as possible in their "natural state." You may thus see for yourselves the differences in the formulation of the questions. You may also see the similarities, and be reminded that all these questions go around the real question, the question we cannot formulate, which asks for the most profound intimacy with ourselves—the living question.

Emma Edwards

OTHER WORKS BY JEAN KLEIN

In English:
    I Am
    Be Who You Are
    The Ease of Being
    Who Am I?
    Open to the Unknown

In French:
    L'ultime Réalité
    Sois ce que tu es
    La Joie sans Objet
    L'insondable Silence

In German:
    Friede im Sein

In Dutch:
    Gesprekken met Jean Klein

In Spanish:
    La Escucha Creativa
    La Mirada Inocente
    La Sencillez del ser
    La Alegria Sin Objeto
    Quien Soy Yo

Translations also available in Italian, Greek and Hebrew

Journals edited by Jean Klein:
    Listening
    Etre (France)
    Essere (Italy)
    Ser (Spain)

Videotapes:
    The Current of Love (with Lilias Folan)
    The Flame of Being (with Michael Toms)
    Love and Marriage (with Paul & Evelyn Moschetta)

Table of Contents

PROLOGUE

I WOULD LIKE TO TALK ABOUT THE EVENTS *which led up to the awakening in your true nature. To begin at the beginning of this historical journey, would you mind talking a little about your childhood? Was it happy? Were you always serious, even as a little boy, or did you have the feelings, actions and reactions of other little boys?*

I had a very happy childhood. When I was very young, I lived in Brno, in what was then Bohemia. Then my father was transferred to Prague and later Vienna.

Did you live in the city or the country?

The city, but we went to the country often. My grandfather had a farm in Bohemia and I went there every summer and loved riding the horses.

What was the atmosphere in your home like? Were your parents religious or spiritual people?

It was a very harmonious house. My parents loved music, paintings and sculpture. My paternal grandfather played the viola very well. No, they were not especially religious people, but they lived very much in aesthetic appreciation.

What about your early education, did you go to the local school?

Yes, but I was more serious than my playmates and enjoyed being on my own a lot. I didn't like competitive sports, for example, and tried by every method to avoid them! My close friends were always much older than I.

When did you begin the violin?

At around seven years. There was always music in our lives and I loved music from infancy. My maternal uncle was a very good amateur guitarist and when I was six he bought me a guitar and gave me lessons for nine months. I enjoyed it very much and practiced a lot. But at that time there was not so much music for the guitar and so my father gave me a violin. I took to it at once and was earnest in my practice. I have continued to play all my life.

Around the age of fourteen or fifteen I began, like many teenagers, to feel a strong urge for freedom. It was a desire to be free from all restraints, all conditions. I lived in constant crisis.

Crisis is a strong word. What do you mean?

Crisis may be too strong a term. I do not mean a psychological, depressive crisis—but a crisis in the sense of always being open to change, to the new, to being surprised. I lived in constant questioning; I began to inquire into many things, always with the inner need to understand how I functioned. I first began reading mystical writings in the Judeo-Christian traditions. Then my explorations turned more towards society. At this time I was very influenced by the ideas of Gandhi on non-violence, and also by the anarchism and ideas on autonomy of Max Stirner and John Henry Mackay. One could say it was a period of anarchism on every level, but always creative, never destructive. First I was interested in how I lived with myself and then how I lived in society. I read Nietzsche, Dostoyevsky, anyone who questioned conformity, and I loved Rilke.

And didn't Gandhi's ahimsa ideas influence you to become vegetarian around this time?

Yes, at sixteen, much to my mother's consternation!

Were there moments as a child when you became self-aware, aware of how you functioned? Because very often childhood passes in a kind of nebulous sleeping state and we wake up to being a young adult.

There were many moments of awareness, but my first real insight (*prise de conscience*) was at about nine or ten years old. I was practicing the violin and the dog was whining, interrupting my practice. I picked up something and began to spank it and suddenly, with my arm raised, I saw the eyes of the dog and realized what I was doing. This was the first time I was aware, in a bipolar way, of my reaction, and of the impact of my reaction. I realized that the reaction was based on a sense of superiority which didn't exist. The impact was very strong. Never again did I fall into *that* trap.

The first glimpse of oneness or self-awareness was at about seventeen. I was waiting one warm afternoon for a train. The platform was deserted and the landscape sleepy. It was silent. The train was late, and I waited without waiting, very relaxed and free from all thinking. Suddenly a cock crowed and the unusual sound made me aware of my silence. It was not the objective silence I was aware of, as often happens when one is in a quiet place and a sudden sound throws into relief the silence around. No, I was ejected into my own silence. I felt myself in awareness beyond the sound or the silence. Subsequently, this feeling visited me several times.

When did you begin to be interested specifically in Eastern philosophy?

My interest in oriental philosophy had been originally sparked by Gandhi. But, at this period, many people were interested also in

Lao Tze, Chuang Tzu, Tagore. Eastern philosophy was in the air. I had friends who were in the Theosophical Society and we discussed metaphysical questions. I always found the Society too sentimental, lacking precision in its thinking, but we had some lively discussions. Then a copy of *The Symbolism of the Cross* by René Guénon fell into my hands and it was a turning point for me.

In which way?

Up until then I had been influenced mostly by non-structural ideas, as I said. I was profoundly anarchistic. But Guénon presented a structure which appealed to me immensely because it was a metaphysical structure, not a political or social structure. It was, for me, an introduction to cosmology. He spoke about becoming an integrated being and referred to Tradition.

As opposed to traditional?

Yes. For Guénon, Tradition is the principle transmitted from master to disciple through initiation. This awoke in me the feeling that it was actually humanly possible to become integrated in the whole.

Did anyone else influence you at this time?

I read Coomaraswamy, especially his arguments with Guénon's view of Buddhism, which caused Guénon to modify his position. I read Aurobindo and in 1929 I heard about Krishnamurti and how he left the Theosophical Society.

Were you touched by his leaving the Theosophical Society?

I was interested in his motive for leaving, I sympathized with him. There was never a time when I wanted to adopt a philosophy or system of ideas, beliefs. I read in order to understand myself more deeply. I had always been interested in function, in the relation between biology and psychology.

Yes, it seems that you were, from an early age, interested in how you, the human being, functioned—the relationship between biology and psychology. Was it this that led you to the study of medicine?

Yes, my love was music and I studied medicine to make my father happy! But it worked out well because my studies combined the two, biology and psychology, the relation between thought, feeling and muscle action. My life was very intense before the war but my inquiry, though sincere, was still around the personality. It was not until my mid-thirties that I became oriented, free from all that former dispersion!

When you were in India?

Even before I went.

And where were you during the Second World War?

In Algeria and France.

During the war years, did your inquiry continue?

Yes. But of course it was difficult in Algeria, and relations with people in France were not easy, because of my activities at the time. But I never stopped self-exploration.

What were those activities?

Let us simply say that they belonged to the right acting of people fleeing oppression.

Did you continue your music?

Yes, in my free time I played three or four chamber concerts a year. And I organized a children's choir in which my two young daughters sang. I also gave music lessons.

And did you meet anyone interesting in the spiritual field at this time?

I met an Englishman who was a disciple of Sai Baba [Sai Baba from Bombay] and he talked to me about the different techniques of transformation practiced in India.

What led you to India after the war? Was it to be in a society where there was Tradition, transmission of the truth?

Yes. For me India was a country which integrated the social and spiritual in daily life. My going was not to find fulfillment in India especially, but to be in an environment that welcomed inquiring. I realized that I would not find what I was looking for in pursuing learning and experiences. I was also completely fed up with the materialism in Europe which was particularly strong after the war. I could perhaps have gone to another country where there was a traditional way of living, but India attracted me. My reading of René Guénon was certainly behind this.

What was your state of mind in this pre-India period? Was this the time when you became oriented, when your inquiry became more focused?

Yes, because I had not found freedom and peace in objects and situations I came to a stop of accumulating knowledge and experience and was brought to a very deep inquiry: How can I find fulfillment, if not in objects? I lived for a long time with this question, in not-knowing.

There was a giving-up of everything which was not essential, which did not refer to inner beauty, inner freedom. I felt enormous energy and intelligence in this period. This brought a joy in living, an enthusiasm for life and great earnestness in the inquiry. It awoke in me the desire to become established in this not-knowing, to find some assistance in the inquiry.

So would you say that the difference between the intelligence before and after this period of intense inquiry was that whereas before, intelligence was related to knowing, later it was related to not-knowing?

Yes, exactly. I had always been a serious inquirer, but now I was a disciple of life, of truth. It was a time of many insights and the spontaneous transposition of these onto all levels of existence. It kept the flame alight.

You said you wanted assistance in the inquiry. What was the motive for this desire to find a guide?

There was still a lack of total fulfillment and I felt my search was still conditioned by the belief in a seeker. I knew consciousness related to objects but not consciousness free from objects. I had no image of what form the assistance would take, man or woman, dream or bird. I was simply open to life, waiting without undertaking anything, for what life would present. And then I felt a certain call to go to India.

So when you went to India you were not conditioned by the idea of gurus and disciples?

Not at all! Not at all!

Did you know anyone in India?

I took a certain number of introductions to people with me.

Gurus or intellectuals?

No, not gurus. Artists, teachers, intellectuals, people generally interested in all the aspects of life. I also had an introduction from Mrs. Lansberry, who was the head of the Buddhist Society in Paris, to a Theravadin *bhikku* in Ceylon and he was the first person I contacted.

How long were you in Ceylon?

Well, before we went to India, the boat stopped in Colombo. I loved Ceylon at once. There was no violence anywhere. You could touch the silence. I found it so beautiful, the temples and the great golden reclining Buddha! And as I had this introduction to the Venerable Rahula, the head of a Theravadin *sangha* (order), during my two weeks in Ceylon we met often and talked. He impressed me quite well and when, a few months later, I was installed in Bangalore (I had been given the address there of a musician, a vina player and singer), I wrote to him. He wrote back and surprised me by saying he was coming to Bangalore to see me. When he arrived, I was at a concert listening to my friend's beautiful voice. Someone told me that Venerable Rahula was outside waiting for me. I went to greet him and invited him into the concert. But he would not come in. He thought music was a distraction. Though I stayed outside with him, I was not happy with this narrow point of view. Again I felt a restriction and a feeling of a lack of freedom. We talked about it over the next few days, but he could not answer my inner question satisfactorily: a distraction from what and for whom? I instinctively felt that all beauty was an expression of the one Beauty.

We exchanged a few letters after that, but I didn't forget this big deception. He presented an inner life of beauty but refused its expressions.

It seems, then, that you already had a strong feeling of truth, freedom, inner discrimination, because you were not taken by his argument, appearance and personality or his ritualistic living.

Yes.

So you lived in Bangalore for some time?

Yes. About three years. I met many interesting people. What surprised me was that while in France, after the war, the conversation turned around good food and fine objects; in India, even though it was such a poor country, no one spoke of these things. The conversation was about spiritual life, dreams and beauty in general.

And you weren't tempted by all the well-known teachers in the south of India?

No, I was not especially interested in finding a teacher. I didn't think about it. Life was my teacher. There were many well-known teachers, but their popularity, far from attracting me, repulsed me.

That reminds me of Abbot Zeno, one of the desert fathers who said, "Do not become the disciple of a man with a great name."

Absolutely! He was quite right!

How then did you meet your "unknown teacher"?

Some of the friends I met, and with whom I spoke of peace, freedom and joy, had a spiritual guide. One day I met their teacher and on this and several other meetings, I asked him many questions, questions that expressed all my earnestness to find my real center.

It seems that you trusted him at once.

I was open to him. I was struck by his lack of striving, his humility. He never tried to impress or convince. There was simply no personality. All his answers came from nowhere, no one, and yet his gentle openness was apparent. I was struck too by his argument that potentially you are, it only needs actualizing. He never saw anyone as not knowing. He gave no hold to my personality.

He gave me many answers, but during the several weeks that I didn't see him I became aware that all my questions had been an escape, an evasion of the real question. The existential crisis I had always lived in became acute. I lived with this feeling that I had missed the real question, a question I was not able to formulate. Then I had the opportunity to visit him where he lived in a little room in the Sanskrit College at Bangalore where he was a teacher. Two other young Indians were present and they were talking about the *Karikas* of Gaudapada and the *Mandukya Upanishad*. The talk was of the four states, waking, sleeping, dreaming and *turiya* (the absence of objects). He said that *turiya* is not properly speaking a state which one enters and leaves. It becomes a non-state (*turiya-citta*) when you are awake in it. It is the absence of ourself which is our total presence. Then there was a silence, the other students left and he suddenly looked at me and asked, "Do you know yourself?" I was a bit disturbed by this question because I didn't really know what he meant. I couldn't find a way to look at it. I said hesitatingly, "Yes," because I was thinking I knew my body, senses and mind very well. He said to me, "You are the knower of your body, senses and mind, but the knower can never be known, because you are it and there's nobody to know it. It can never become an object of observation because it is your totality." This saying had a very strong impact on me. I had a glimpse of reality in this moment because it stopped all intellectual faculties. We were silent and I left.

And did this impact remain with you when you got home?

It left a very strong echo in me of freedom from old beliefs. I went home and lived with it free from all conceptualization and felt myself awake in this not-knowing. It was completely new, there was no absence of knowing.

Did life change or go on as usual?

Life went on, eating, meeting people. But there was now a feeling that I was behind all daily activities. I saw Pandiji many times afterwards and realized that he was my guru because this profound impact could only come from a guru. So you see he found me when I was not looking for him!

Were you at any point in the quest convinced that you would one day know your real nature?

Yes. After the first meeting with him in Bangalore. I never formulated it. It was never a goal. The word "enlightenment" never entered my thoughts. Pandiji certainly didn't use the term. It was simply a lively feeling, without formulation, of being free from myself, free from all restrictions, all ideas, free from the knowing of freedom.

Did you ever spend a lot of time together, live together?

Yes. For three or four months.

Is it important to live with the guru?

No, it's not important. He stayed in my house purely for practical reasons.

How did you spend the time together?

He was teaching at the college all day. Sometimes we ate together and every morning he knocked on my door very early and we sat together in silence. Sometimes we spoke about the scriptures, because, being a man of tradition, he very often referred his sayings to the scriptures. But he never did so arbitrarily. Each time he spoke this way, it was exactly the moment when I needed to know it. There was really a feeling of oneness. I was not aware of a "me" and a "he" in our being together. There was real love, not in the way we are accustomed to mean it. It was the most exalted being in love. His presence was continually drenched with warm feeling.

Did he ever transmit to you through touch?

That was not his way with me. We communicated mostly through the eyes. Sometimes he touched my shoulder or hand, but our closeness was closer than all touching.

We also walked together. He was an admirer and this appealed to my artistic nature. He loved music and singing and could imitate the sound of any bird.

Were there any disciplines or exercises that he taught you during this time?

Only to be aware of when conditioning comes in in daily life. He emphasized the problem of day-dreaming and strategy-building. He also emphasized that one should never push away conditioning but only see it clearly, and he reminded me to constantly refer to the first insight, the first non-experience.

You mean, to remember it?

Go knowingly in it, not remember it intellectually. It is presence, not a memory.

Did he teach you any yoga exercises?

No, it was not on the program! When we were sitting together he occasionally made me aware of certain patterns. I knew a few yoga postures already and, if he found me doing them, he sometimes corrected them. Mostly, we sat. Our togetherness, our meditation was never intentional. He emphasized only awareness free from objects and not to try to become a better man. Doing things was a defense for him. His presence was all that was needed—and his sayings, the way he brought the truth to me through words which emphasized the silence. He emphasized the silence after the sayings, the silence in which understanding becomes alive, free from the words.

Was he in your thoughts very often?

I did not think of him because I could not personify, objectify him. There was a deep feeling of oneness. I was not at all attached to his physical being. Everything he gave was a pearl. I took it as a pearl and lived with it.

There were many moments when we were just happy to be together, not talking, not thinking. His presence was my presence and my presence was his presence. His being was the transmission. In a real teacher this is all transmission is. Any intentional transmission is sentimentality, romanticism.

You have often said that you like to be pushed into the corner with questions. Did you do this with your teacher? Did you ask many questions?

Oh yes, many questions! These brought us to the edge of thinking. They exhausted thinking.

Were your questions ever of a practical nature, how to conduct your daily life and so on?

Almost never. I tried to use all my knowledge to solve the problem myself. I had a very great veneration for him and when I really looked at my feelings, I did not want to bother him with things I could solve myself. I left my time with him for other questions.

Would you mind my asking whether you remember any of the questions you asked him?

From time to time I would ask about spontaneity, or about thinking and how it functions in complementarity, how I could not think of light without reference to dark, and so on. So I asked him how I could go beyond complementarity, beyond thinking, how I could go beyond "to be or not to be."

You obviously have a very good intellect. Would you say your questions were intellectual?

As you say, my intellect was a very good tool and I used it, but my questions arose not from the mind but from my existential conflict. As I had a strong intellect, I went as far as possible with my questions. For me the intellect was a vital element in the search. Sometimes he answered me in the form of a question which gave me no hold. He pushed me to the edge of the thinkable. Sometimes he did not answer verbally and that silent answer was even more tangible.

Would you say your approach was more jnani *than* bhakti, *more the way of knowledge than devotion?*

Yes. Not so much *bhakti*, of course. But all my questions were carried by love. It was never a dry, mental exercise. He also had a great intellect. Traditionally, when you are a pandit there is nothing you must not know. (laughs)

But you can only come to knowledge when there is love, unconditional adoration.

Were you ever curious about him, about his life, his role as a teacher or as a man, possibly as a husband or father, how he related to other students and so on?

No, never. I never asked personal questions and I never spoke personally about him. It was a sacred relationship. It was a profoundly serious togetherness. I never doubted his integrity for a moment.

At this time, even though you knew intellectually that there was nothing to achieve, did you still feel and function as if there was?

No. There was no thought at all of becoming or attaining. The most I could say would be that perhaps there was still a residue of eccentric energy, energy to become. But every time I was with Pandiji, his presence channeled the energy that was dispersed.

Then it is important to spend some time with the teacher?

Oh, yes.

Because you often downplay this . . .

It is not the duration which is important, but the quality of the time together.

So the fact that you were with your teacher for about three years, that Krishna Menon met his teacher for maybe forty minutes and that some people have known you for twenty years or more has nothing to do with igniting the spark? But can one be too long a "student"?[1]

It is not a question of time. It can happen at any moment in life. But there are people who have a slow intellect, slow understanding, or who are stuck in the garage. It can also be that they have such conditioned minds through years of wrong training that the mind has lost its subtlety and is the same as a slow mind.

---

[1] For more on this subject, see the article "The Guru and the Disciple" in the December 1989 issue of *Listening,* a publication of the Jean Klein Foundation, P.O. Box 2111, Santa Barbara, CA 93102.

You had, I believe, at this time some freedom from family and financial obligations.

Yes. I had previously organized my life to make this possible.

You are aware that many people wonder whether to organize their lives to be more free from their obligations and social responsibilities. Do you think that a serious inquirer into truth should do this?

One should do all in one's power to realize this for some time. It usually means foregoing material wealth, letting go of a way of living, living in the most functional way: food and sleep.

We often hear, "First I will make money and then I will retire and devote myself to truth-seeking."

This comes from the calculating mind. It is a statement from complete ignorance. There is nothing functional in this reasoning. It is only a postponing. The right moment does not come from the mind. When you feel the urge to leave the competitive world, the desire is very strong. You don't, of course, avoid your family responsibilities, but you see them in a different way. The reasoning to make enough money to retire on is an escape from what belongs to the immediate moment.

But what if one has several children, for example, and simply cannot change one's job?

What is important is that you feel the inner need *to be*. Then your surroundings—what belongs to you—arrange themselves accordingly. Existence on this earth gives everyone the opportunity to know Life and to be awake in Life. What we are looking for is our nearest.

I am interested to know why, though your teacher never emphasized yoga, you pursued your study of it, presumably because you still had an interest in the relation between biology and psychology. Was this why you went to learn yoga with Krishnamacharya?

Yes. But I was not at all attracted to yoga from the exercise or gymnastic point of view. I wanted to become more conscious of the body. I wanted the body to become more subtle, more energized, more expanded. It was for the love of feeling the body elastic and receptive. And he was a lovely man to meet.

Was this before or after the awakening?

Oh, before.

And how did you meet Dibianandapuri?

On a bus in Bangalore. He was in a state of *mauna* (not speaking). We got out at the same station and he took a little blackboard out of his dhoti and wrote asking me where I came from and that he felt I was his brother. I said, "How can it be otherwise?" Then he wrote, "If you have the time, let us go for a walk." So we walked and talked (he with his blackboard). He was living in a little Siva temple outside Bangalore and we met often. He was originally from Puri and had lived a long time in Kashmir. We talked about the Kashmir teachings, how they emphasize the energy body not the physical body. This was my main concern. I was already aware of the energy body and regarded it, and not the bone-muscle structure, as the real body. Dibianandapuri confirmed and expanded my intuition and experience. He gave the energy body priority and showed me how all postures could be done independently of the physical body.

Did you see other teachers on the level of Pandiji while you were in India?

I saw Krishna Menon four or five times later on, and found him highly able in *vidya vritti*, the formulation of what cannot be formulated. Absolutely a beautiful being.

And Ramana Maharshi?

Unfortunately I never met him because he passed away a few months before I arrived in India.

So while you were a disciple of Pandiji's you were never drawn to other teachers for clarification?

There was no desire at all in me for that. I didn't go to India to find a teacher. The teacher found me. There's only one teacher. I quickly came to the conviction that there is nothing to teach and that what you are looking for doesn't belong to any teaching or "teacher." So why look for anyone? It is the presence of the guru that shows there is nothing to teach because the teacher is established in the "I am." So I realized that only the "I am," not a mind or a body, can bring you to the "I am."

How long did you live in this way, seeing Pandiji?

For about three years.

And then you left Bangalore and went to Bombay?

Yes, I went sightseeing.

And during this stay there was the moment of enlightenment?

Yes, it was a total switch-over from the residual conditioned state to the unconditioned state. Awareness expanded completely and I felt myself in globality.

Had this happened before?

No. There had been glimpses, but this was more than a glimpse. There was no going back. I had found my real ground.

Did you know in the moment itself that it would be permanent or did you discover this in the days that followed?

Because of the quality of the switch-over there was no doubt that I could be again taken by duality, and this was confirmed in the days and weeks that followed. I felt a rectification in my body and in my brain, as if all the parts had found their right place, their most comfortable position. I saw all daily events spontaneously appearing in the non-state, in my total absence, real presence.

Could you say what were the exact conditions, physical and mental, before this moment: The Threshold?

There had been, for two years, a retreat of all the energy commonly used in becoming, so that when some flying birds crossed my horizon, instead of becoming lost in them, they were lost in me and I found myself in awareness free from all objects. This time what I admired, the birds, dissolved in my admiring, in presence. And admiring dissolved in the Admired. Before the birds appeared, I had been in a profound and prolonged state of being open to openness. Now I found myself *as* the openness, identical with openness. Openness was my being. There was no more duality.

Was there any other difference between this time and other times when you had looked at birds?

Before, there was still a looker looking at something. This was a moment when there was simply looking without a looker. Previously, it had become my nature to live in pure perception with objects, not living in the divided mind. I had for a long time ignored the arising of all qualifications.

Ignored?

It belongs to the traditional approach, and so that of my teacher, never to refuse or indulge the coming up of qualifications, but simply to ignore, and eventually forget them. Neither to look for freedom nor avoid non-freedom. The mind simply ceased to play a role except in a purely functional way.

So in a certain way you were ripe for the moment?

In other words the moment was waiting for me!

How is life different now?

There is no more identification with time and space, body, senses and mind. All events happen in awareness.

Did your relationships change?

There was no more relationship. As there's no longer an "I," there is not another.

Can this non-state be described at all?

It is love where the mind is dissolved in love.
(long pause)

Were you in a hurry to return to Bangalore to see Pandiji?

No. I enjoyed my total freedom, freedom from all doing. I postponed all projects and stayed in Bombay another week or so.

How was your next meeting with Pandiji? Was it full of tears of joy and gratitude?

He was never absent, so there was no hurry to see him. He never acknowledged or mentioned anything, though he recognized a change. I could tell from his way of speaking. He would never talk about it and risk making a state of it. Quite frankly, tears and emotion after an insight show that it is a state. As for gratitude, there was from the beginning gratitude to him. There was no emotivity in our meeting, only joyful togetherness, and an un-voiced laughter that the seeker *is* the sought and is always so very, very near.

What stimulated your return to Europe?

I could have remained and taught in India, but I felt I belonged in a way to Europe and I was quite interested in going back to see from this new unqualified vision what I had previously seen and qualified. Also Pandiji suggested I return because he felt the West needed me. In a way his role was played for me. We knew we would always have being and friendship in common. There was no reason to stay. So I left my best friend and a country I loved.

And how did you find Europe? This must have been in about 1957, yes?

Yes. I found a total absence of sacredness, an absence of love. I found hate and competition, demanding and asking. I remember feeling, "Is there any hope for these people to discover life? Is there a spark there?" The materialism seemed the same as it was before I went to India, but now I saw it more clearly and saw its cause.

It sounds a depressing situation to come back to!

No, not depressing. Depressing for whom? It was simply a fact. I saw things as they were without any qualification. It was clear to me that these facts were produced by the identification with what we ultimately are not.

And did seeing things as they are inspire you to teach, and did you find a spark?

As long as there is a human being, there's a spark. Even in the murderer are moments when he's not a murderer. Seeing the cause awakened the teaching in me.

How did you begin teaching?

People came to me. I have never taken myself for a teacher, so I never solicited students. The teacher only appears when asked to teach.

When did you introduce the teaching about the body, and why?

About a year after I returned from India I found it necessary to expand the teaching to the psychosomatic level. It became apparent, through meeting people, that identification with what we are not is confirmed and reinforced by contraction on the psychosomatic level. The I-concept is only a contraction on the level of the body-mind. It has no more reality than a bad habit. It is a defense against being nobody.

In getting to know the body-mind, one can discover more clearly the nature of the identification, and so let it go. The relaxed body is a relaxed mind. In a relaxed body and mind you are open to receiving, available, welcoming, open to the openness. The relaxed, light, energetic, sattvic body-mind are a near expression of your real nature. It is almost impossible for a conditioned body-mind to be receptive to truth, open to grace. It can happen that truth pierces through all conditioning since the insight into our true nature ultimately has nothing to do with the body or the mind. But it is exceedingly rare. My teaching also on the level of the body was only to make discrimination more likely and to help more of my friends be available to global insight. Of course, I also spontaneously taught all I knew, which included knowledge of the body. But it was really about availability.

And how do you find the West more than thirty years after your return?

Still mainly living on the level of competition, quantity and becoming. But there are poetic moments, moments of beauty.

Do you regard yourself as coming from a lineage of masters?

In a certain way, yes. The way of approaching truth belongs to a certain current, but there are no entities in a line.

So you were not interested in who was the teacher of your teacher?

In the teaching of my guru I saw the teaching of his guru, but when the teaching is strong there is no reference to the past. There is only eternal presence. What does "lineage" mean? It is still a someone looking for security in a something.

Do you regard yourself as belonging to a certain tradition?

A tradition of truth-seekers. *Advaita* is not a system, a religion or technique. It is not even a philosophy. It is simply the truth.

And that truth is transmitted without reference to any system or tradition?

Yes.

Your teaching has been compared to that of some Chan masters, to Chuang Tzu and Taoist teaching. Do you feel this is a valid comparison?

Yes, because these teachings were only about what one is not and this opens the disciple to the truth of what he is. It is only accidentally that I call the current of my teaching *Advaita*.

We live in troubled times and the reign of quantity as you said. Do you think there is hope for humankind?

There is not only hope, there is the certainty that we will one day live in beauty. We come from beauty and beauty cannot but look for beauty.

Baak, Holland

October 1988

Huize Mariapoli retreat center is pleasant, light, well-organized and friendly, welcoming laughs and silences without qualification. In the lake in front of the white manor house, trees are reflected and, at this time of year, the ground is colored by fallen leaves. The quiet little red brick village with its tidy gardens and clock-tower spire, suddenly bursts into the annual harvest festival with brass bands and flower floats.

The earth is flat, absorbed by the vast translucent sky. Canals, cows, trees, white clouds, all objects find their perfect setting. In this space and light the artist in us awakes. We visit, in the forests of Otterlo, the Kroller-Muller Art Gallery, which houses one of the greatest collections of van Gogh and an impressive sculpture garden.

The silence of our meetings in the high-pitched barn is made known to us by the falling of chestnuts on the roof. Our timelessness is revealed by the punctuality of the bells...

LISTENING IS OUR BASIC NATURE. We are more or less accustomed to listening to an object, to our surroundings and to our nearest environment: body, senses and mind. But I speak today of this listening where there is nothing to listen to.

You can never think this listening, you can never objectify it, you can never fix it; and in listening there's not a listener, there's no place for a listener, for a controller, a doer, for an enjoyer, for a sufferer. Listening is free from all furniture, from all memory. It is a non-state. In a state you go in and come out; listening is a continuum. When you are listening to your body, senses and mind, then your listening is completely open; there's no grasping, no taking. The perceived comes directly to your openness.

One can say that every object heard brings you back to your homeground, to listening. When the perception is sustained so that the concept does not arise, then the perceived brings you back to your listening. Listening in the beginning may be understood as a brain function, but it doesn't belong to a specific organ, an ear. So when the listening is sustained, then it becomes awareness, lucidity. Listening is constant meditation, without a meditator or an object of meditation.

This may be the content of our dialogue.

Is it possible to stay in that listening when you are working in a way that demands some concentration?

You must first discover this unconditioned listening before any activity. Then you will see that every activity comes directly out of listening and vanishes in listening, and finally you will become established in this listening even during activity. Listening is behind all perceptions. It is the light which gives reality to all that is perceived. It can never become an object. And, of course, there is no place for an independent entity; in listening you live really your complete absence. You can only feel your presence in your total absence.

Is this listening the same as consciousness? Is consciousness in the brain?

Listening and consciousness are not in the brain.

But what is happening in the moment when you are no longer in that listening? Are you emotionally bound or involved? Do you identify with objects?

You cannot help it, you *are* listening. See also that you turn away from listening and you identify yourself with your personality; you go into a state of restriction. You must see it in the moment itself. When you see it in the moment itself, there's a stop. It is this stop which brings you back to listening, or rather, this stop *is* the listening. So first see that you objectify yourself constantly, that you think of yourself as a woman, as this personality with this history and that future and so on. It is all a figment of the mind.

What is important is to really be aware of how you feel when your brain is free from all representation. You are nowhere, there is no center, there is no border, there's only space, you *are* the space. So go with it, live with it, don't leave it an intellectual understanding.

If I am not allowed to go back to my intellect, how can I remember things?

I am not saying that you cannot use your intellect; but to understand what you really are, you must follow the real mind, that is, the higher reasoning. Of course you need a certain kind of reasoning in the objective world, but when you want to discover the ultimate subject, you need higher reasoning.

Is higher reasoning beyond everyday reasoning?

Yes. You must have an intuitive glimpse of what is being said here, a fore-feeling. This glimpse is not in the head. You live too much in your head. The fore-feeling is on every level of your psychosomatic structure; the understanding must be body understanding.

If someone does what he feels without thinking, his surroundings will probably not accept him.

Make your question clear for yourself. First live with the question. When you really ask yourself a question, it comes from the answer. You are not able to ask a question without already in some way having the answer. The question comes from the answer, so live with your question, wait. You must wait without waiting for the answer to appear in the question; wait without grasping, without taking, without concluding. Be totally open to the answer; the answer will come only in your complete openness. The answer never comes from the brain, the brain knows only the already known.

What can you do to not bring down to an intellectual level that which you feel by intuition?

First listen, and in the listening you will see that you don't listen. In *your* listening there is expectation. You are listening with anticipation. See that. It is a fact, without judging or comparison, it is a fact. Seeing really the fact that you don't listen brings you to listening and listening is the answer. Feel yourself in the answer. To live freely in the answer you must give up what is not the answer. But don't emphasize what you give up; emphasize the giving-up, the up-giving, itself.

5

That is the answer, the living answer. In living in the giving-up you are completely free. *You* don't give up, it gives up itself. It is not a process of volition. It really works. (laughter)

It seems when I am in that state of listening I have no emotions, no feelings, is that so?

You are completely open. There is no emotivity, only a feeling: that is love.

But how is it that these moments of insight are so short? You want them to last!

When you first have this insight you must live with it from moment to moment, like a mother lives with her child, like a painter lives with his painting, like a musician. A musician is a musician every moment.

If surroundings are only connected to the person, what happens when the person disappears as a person?

When the person disappears you are in connection with reality; only then are you in connection with reality. As long as you live identified with your personality, you make an object of yourself and live in relationship from object to object. When you are free from personality, free from this identification with an object, all your surroundings refer to your totality, refer to your globality. Without the interference of the ego, you really see the facts. Relationship becomes relationless. The background of every relationship is then love. So-called relationship between objects is only looking for security; there's only asking. But what is important is that you see it in life as it occurs, in the moment itself. When you really see that you are only looking for security and approval, look inwards and ask: What is my reaction at this moment? You may have an awareness of futility, a tragic feeling because you have lived only with images, repeating images. You have lived with surroundings which are more or less furniture; the people in your life are like furniture too.

6

Is it true that in the beginning it takes a lot of inspiration? It is difficult to be in this listening because you are always distracted by your surroundings, by the things you do?

For whom is it difficult? See simply that you don't listen. What happens in the moment you see that you don't listen? You feel yourself out of the process of not listening. This moment is very important. It is not even a moment, it is timeless. This timeless moment refers to itself; live in it knowingly, be completely attuned to it.

You said that the living experience would repeat itself and would be more frequent?

Yes.

What is the difference between such an experience, the experience that we don't live consciously, and that moment which is between two thoughts or perceptions?

Looking for meditation, looking for peace, comes out of the experience of deep sleep. When the body wakes up in the morning, there is still the residue of this experience in deep sleep. This residue is in the moments between deep sleep and the waking state when the body is not completely awake. Be completely attuned to these moments. It is a state of admiring. Attune yourself completely to this admiring state where there is no admirer and nothing admired.

Even though you see you are not listening and you see that there are still thousands of imaginings, when does everything come to that stop you are talking about?

First see that you don't listen. Experience that you don't listen. It is an important moment you have never had. Everything you say is memory, which has nothing to do with experience. You speak from memory; you have not listened, you have thought, and there's no experience in thinking. When you see this you will come to a state

7

of "I don't know." It is a state where you are completely helpless. You must fully live this state of helplessness.

Has a child the possibility of being in the listening you speak of?

A child is in constant discovery.

Why is it that we can't continue being like the child who lives in constant discovery? Or when we are in listening, do we come back to that state of the child? If so, could we simply follow the child, imitate the child, if we have a child?

When you observe a child, the child is in constant discovering. The child lives from moment to moment. It does not look for any profit or becoming; it enjoys each moment completely. Yes, you may observe the child and the observation of the child may bring you to some conclusion.

I do not exactly understand what I have to listen to.

You already know yourself in listening to your body, your agitation, your fear, your anxiety. But you don't know yourself in objectless listening where there's nothing to listen to, where there's only listening, only openness. Where are you when you are in love? Then the somebody completely disappears and there's only love, objectless love. Then you love for the sake of love. This is listening, it is presence.

You said that listening has nothing to do with the brain or with the body. Is it so that it has nothing to do with being born, or with the dying of the body?

It is inherent to the brain to listen. Attention is a natural function of the brain. And when the attention is sustained it expands—for want of a better phrase—into consciousness. You don't listen with your specific organ, the ear, you listen with your whole body. Listening has never been born, it will never die, listening is. But don't be stuck to the word listening. Do you see what I mean?

Is it the same as when you listen to somebody playing the guitar and it is only after the listening that you realize what the music did to you? You have the intense feeling of the music, after listening.

The aesthetic joy is after the hearing of the music. Then you are really one with the music.

Is it not also during the listening to the music?

I would say that it is not then full listening, because the music appears in time, appears in addition. We can see the whole picture of a Rembrandt in the museum, but we can never grasp it with one look. There's a kind of addition of one look to another. There may be seventeen looks, and only in the end can you say there is the joy in the picture. But then, in the moment of joy, the picture, as a perception, is no longer there. One cannot feel the joy with the representation; joy comes after the perception.

So if you don't use the word listening, could you say that to listen and to see are the same?

You must make a little inner effort to transpose the word listening. Listening is seeing.

I don't agree at all. It seems to me that one enjoys music while one is listening to it. When you are listening to Schubert you are in love with it while it is happening. You don't suddenly enjoy it when it is over.

Music, like every art, points to your real nature, but in this enjoyment there is not an enjoyer. This enjoying is no longer in subject-object relationship. There's only enjoying.

Yes, but that's being listening. It seems that we are talking about two different things. What you are talking about now is actually being, whereas this knowing something after it happened is not being, it's something mechanical or intellectual or of the ego.

Every object to which you listen brings you back to listening, because the listened is a projection of listening. The projected has its homeground in listening. When the projected comes back to its homeground it discovers its nature, which is listening. That is really being.

Could you give me a simple example of something projected?

You see a flower. The moment you see the flower there's only seeing, you are not thinking "that is a flower." If you do think, there is no more seeing at that moment. So when looking at a flower there is only looking; there is no more flower at all, there's only seeing. But you are not aware of this seeing. You become aware the moment the seen, which is a projection of the seeing, comes back to the seeing. Then there is an experience without an experiencer. So every object seen, heard, touched, can bring you back to your homeground which is pure seeing, hearing, touching. At first it appears as multidimensional attention, but when the attention is sustained for any reason, then it expands into awareness. First you are aware of something and then this something returns to awareness, to its homeground, and what remains is objectless awareness which knows itself by itself. When we use a word like listening or hearing or seeing, it is here the same as prayer. Praying is waiting, waiting without waiting.

What happens in the moment after seeing the flower when I say, "I loved seeing the flower"?

Consciousness and its object are one. An object has no reality in itself, no reality outside consciousness. It depends on consciousness. So when you see a flower and there is only seeing, the flower is in agreement within you and me. But the enjoyment of the beauty, the joy, is after the flower. It comes when the flower has referred you back to the seeing, to your own beauty. The flower points directly to your looking, a looking where there's no looker, no seer. There is only seeing, only looking. Yes, the aesthetic joy is after the looking, after the seeing.

The flower is perceived and conceived. It is perceived with the five senses and conceived with the sixth sense. Generally the conceiving comes too quickly, so you must sustain looking at the flower like an artist, like a poet. Artists perceive the flower, but don't conceive it. They don't conceptualize it; they see it with the five senses. When the perception is sustained, the flower is really allowed to be a flower. All the flowering possibilities are explored. When you look at a flower without superimposing concepts, you are *in* the flowering process. It is a constant spring. I remember when Theo, the brother of Vincent van Gogh, wrote to him about his painting trees like flames and van Gogh replied that he saw the four seasons in one moment. That is a perception, not a conception.

WHEN I TRY TO LISTEN TO MYSELF, *I very often become tired. What can I do?*

You are aware that you are tired, so find out where this tiredness is localized. The word tiredness is not tired, so free yourself from the concept tired and face only the percept. Where is the tiredness in your body? Explore, and then you will see what happens. Write to me. Don't forget.

Is the same answer true if it concerns tension in the head?

Tension in the head is perceived. Take note that you are mainly localized in your head. Accept the perception totally. Go completely with the perception. Don't fight it, don't escape it, go completely with it. Then you are witness to the perception. In witnessing in this way you are no longer an accomplice with the tension in your brain which is a contraction of energy, a reaction. So, as there is no longer an accomplice, you will see the reaction; and, in the seeing, the energy dissolves.

Your body must become an object of your observation. Be a completely innocent observer, without any intention.

Is there a solution to the paradox that we are talking about something that's beyond reasoning but nevertheless we are reasoning about it?

13

We are here concerned with understanding. Understanding means that you clearly see the perspective: that you take yourself for a personal entity, identify yourself with it, and act, think and feel from this point of view. You have objectified yourself, you have given it a name, "Eliza Brown," and you identify yourself with Eliza Brown. You contact your surroundings through Eliza Brown, and it is Eliza Brown who meets Mr. John Smith. Everything around you is in a relation of object to object, concept to concept. Eliza Brown looks constantly for security, to be loved, to be considered, and so on. This you must see, not only hear, not only think, but see in the moment itself. This understanding is necessary. It happens at your age that you see that all your life you have identified yourself with Eliza Brown and that this is the result of your education, your father and mother, society and experiences. But it is all a figment of your imagination. When you really see it, you will say, "I must now become serious." But real understanding is never on the verbal plane. It becomes understanding only in your wholeness, in your completeness. What you have understood dissolves in being the understanding. You will know that this being understanding is silence. The formulation completely vanishes and abides in silence. This understanding is instantaneous, like a flash of insight when you say, "This *is*." It doesn't go through the discriminating mind; it doesn't go through the mind at all.

When I meditate I know that I fix a certain point. I believe I have heard you say to perceive a particular sensation, but when I do this, it fixes it more. So what do I do in this situation?

I remember I told you on that occasion that you should take note that you are fixed in your factory of words and thinking, that you know yourself only in your frontal brain, and that as you live there, there is tension. I told you to be aware of those tensions, go with them, and relax completely. In this relaxation you will be free from tension in your brain. Instead of feeling you are in your head, you feel you are behind, at the base of your skull. There, all the energy is gathered before it strikes the brain and you find the word and

14

open the dictionary to look for the formulation. Once the energy is behind and you have mastered it so that it does not go in front, you will feel it still localized, but behind, not in the right and left brain. But this is only a transition, because the energy will descend to your heart and this is the last door. Then you will find yourself nowhere, because your real presence is when you are nowhere, in your complete absence—absence as a concept and as a percept. So listen to this and forget it immediately.

What we are fundamentally can never be objectified. It cannot be localized in your body. It only becomes apparent in exploring your absence, your total absence. What you are can never be emphasized; it is constantly open, never in conclusion, never in assertion. As soon as you take yourself for somebody there is contraction, there is localization, but when you are completely free from the person, you are expanded in space, you are constantly in meditation.

When you try to meditate you create a state of it, because there is intention, anticipation. You have a goal, you are looking for a result. When there is intention there cannot be any letting-go. It is very clear: as long as there is intention, there's no letting-go.

Dr. Klein, you keep reminding us there is nothing to do and we also keep asking you how to do it. Would you say something about that?

Accept as a principle that there is nothing to attain, because what we are looking for, we are already. What we are looking for is our nearness. What we are looking for is the looker. When you know this, you will feel how every step you take to attain yourself is a going away. Then there is a completely natural giving-up, because there is nothing to gain, nothing to lose. See how this understanding acts on you. You will find yourself, naturally, as you were before you were born.

We do physical exercises, because we want to be in silence, but why don't you give us mental exercises to feel that silence, because we are thinking creatures?

Because there are no exercises at all.

Then why do we do yoga?

Only to make acquaintance with what we are not. Because to know ourselves we must first know what we are not, and to know what we are not, we must first know what it is that we are not. So explore the facts of what you are not, but know how to explore with a completely innocent mind, a listening mind. When you proceed in this way you will one day find yourself in listening.

If we were all in open listening, I have the idea that there would be nothing one could ask for or give. If we were all in that same state it would be very silent.

Yes. There would be spontaneous action. In this non-state there is complete harmony, you are adequate to every situation. Every situation in your life brings with it its own solution, its own answer.

When the situation in which you are living is getting worse . . .?

Ask the question: For whom does it get worse? If it becomes worse it means you have established a personal relationship with the situation. Look at your surroundings from the point of view of openness. Then things come up that you have never seen before. The conflict in your situation is only because you see a fraction, because you situate yourself as a fraction. From your completeness, from your wholeness, from your openness, there's no conflict.

The question is, can one personally help somebody?

If you need help, you are already helped. You have it already. You don't need to ask. But see also that you may refuse it.

If we are not in openness, does that mean that, at that moment, we are refusing help?

Of course. It is the person who refuses. But see that the person is an illusion. You can only free yourself from the person when you understand the nature of the person. The person is cooked up by the mind!

How important is it to think? When we are listening, we don't think.

Who thinks? Is there a thinker? When you need to think in daily, practical life, then think. But there are many long moments when you don't need to think. Your problem is that you are completely absorbed in daydreaming. Daydreaming and anticipating certain situations are exactly the same. It is living in psychological time, going from the past to the future, the future to the past. It is a constant agitation, so you are never in the present. When you really see, from your openness, how it acts on you, there is transmutation. But be aware when there is dreaming during the day. Do you see what I mean?

Yes, I think so.

Do we need help as long as we consider ourselves a person?

Then you need help! (laughter) Do you see it? That only the person needs help, because the person is in insecurity, so it is constantly looking for psychological survival.

Why is it that something that isn't there should be helped?

When you take yourself for a person, you automatically need help.

So if I take myself for a person, I will need some technique or guidance so that I do not stay in the vicious circle of keeping myself as a person?

Any technique or system keeps the person in the vicious circle, because it is trying to heal what is fundamentally an illusion. See that the person has created a universe around him of beliefs and ideas, and looks for techniques and systems to overcome insecurity. The person needs help constantly. And, of course, society proposes many very clever escapes and compensations. Very many books have been written about how to escape from the person, but it is all still in the vicious circle. See it and see what it means to see it.

Really see it. Then you will find yourself outside of the vicious circle. This moment is important because the seer is completely out of what is seen—the seer is free from the seen.

Could it be that we are afraid of the unknown?

Of course. You are afraid of dying. The person is very heavy baggage, but you would rather carry an enormous weight than no weight at all!

Who is the "you" that takes itself for a person?

It is an identification with the personality. Consciousness identifies itself with its object. It is a forgetting.

Consciousness identifies itself with a nothing?

Yes, then you act as a personality. You look at all your surroundings from the point of view of the personality. The mind, at this moment, is split between positive and negative, like and dislike. All your looking is with choice, with selection. You are continually in the becoming process of looking for security, psychological survival, anything which gives you security. If it does, you identify with it. But if it does not give security, you push it away, because your looking is never innocent. The moment that you remain in your completeness, in your openness, there's no division; there is wholeness.

You must see how you function in daily life; it is the only way.

Is it not natural to have certain kinds of security, for example, food for dinner, and lodging? I think it is part of human nature.

You need food for biological survival. But psychological survival is a complete illusion. There are certain countries in our society where biological survival plays an important role, but here in the West, there's only psychological survival, survival for an illusion.

But we keep mixing the two together because we are afraid.

18

Look at your fear; become very familiar with it. You don't really know your fear; you know only your idea of it, your memory. You must face the actual sensation of fear, in the moment itself, when you are in the fear.

Become more sensitive to your body and mind. One must become more and more acquainted with innocent observation. Take note that you don't observe, that you don't observe without qualification. Your observation must be completely open. The observed must come to you because the observed is you. Let it come back to you, let it completely unfold in your observation. Then you will have a right relation with your surroundings, a love relation. The poet knows how to observe, to look at things completely innocently.

*I*F YOU ARE THE WITNESS *how can you be involved with things that are going on in life?*

You are always the witness, so you don't need to try to be the witness. When you try to witness, you objectify what you, in any case, are. There's not a thinker, not a doer, not a sufferer, not an enjoyer; they don't exist. There's enjoying, there's doing, but no one does anything.

If there is no sufferer how would you see real ailment or pain? Does that make medical care in the end superfluous?

Only an object can suffer. Ask who is the knower of the suffering object? Follow my sayings. Have the right representation. It is the shadow which can bring you back to its substance.

What is the difference between your way of functioning and my way of functioning?

You take yourself for somebody, I take myself for nothing: that's the difference. I know myself in nothingness, you know yourself only as John Smith.

But I don't see . . .

You must follow me. You project already, in your next question. You take yourself for John Smith and look around from the point of view of John Smith. Myself, I have no point of view. You choose things which give you security, and if they don't give you security you push them away. For me there is no security or insecurity. But ultimately there's no difference between you and me.

I don't think I properly understood what you were saying yesterday about listening to music and looking at flowers. As soon as you say, "That was a lovely quintet," or ,"That's a beautiful rose," there's no more pleasure, for then it's turned into a concept. But it still seems to me that the enjoyment of beautiful music or a beautiful sight acts in the moment itself and not afterwards.

Look, we have four hundred years of occidental music, and it is a language like any other language. It's a language which manifests itself in time. To really understand a language you must follow it to the end, point by point, addition after addition; and when you have heard the full meaning of the language you can really enjoy it. In the moment of enjoyment there's not an enjoyer, there's only enjoying, which is not in subject-object relationship. It is the same with painting and architecture. It takes a certain number of looks until there's a fusion of one look with another look; when all the looks are one, then there's enjoyment.

In my own experience the actual sound, or the actual sight of a rose is immediate pleasure. With the building I agree . . .

Listening to music is a very high art, because it calls for a capacity of listening that is at the same time horizontal and vertical. It must be without any anticipation, for every moment is a full moment. Even most musicians do not have the capacity for listening to music because there is often anticipation. When you hear music from the 16th or 17th century, you already know the formulation, you anticipate already, you are in a kind of end-gaining. But even when you know the way of formulating and the conclusions in Bach, Mozart, Beethoven, Debussy, Bruchner and Ravel, you still postpone conclusion. You live in not-knowing and enjoy, take pleasure in, the music in hearing it—that's the main thing!

Could you make clear the difference between vertical and horizontal listening?

In the horizontal way you feel the language, you feel the melody, and in the vertical you see how the melody is dressed. There is a difference between the oriental and the occidental way of hearing music. For example, one hears Indian music only on the horizontal plane. When you hear a sound, other sounds appear in you. Oriental music calls for more attention, more participation, to complete the music. But still there is not a hearer, only hearing; there's not a listener, only listening.

Sir, you spoke of enjoyment and it seems we are misunderstanding the word enjoyment in relation to time. Could you say more on that?

In the moment you say, "I enjoy these paintings," or, "I enjoy looking at the cathedral," then at that moment you are not enjoying it because you have already objectified the joy. We have had thousands and thousands of years of humanity, but we have never been able to put joy, peace and love in the frame of space and time. For it is only in your total absence, free from subject-object, that you live joy. It is in your total absence that you live your presence. In this presence is joy, is peace. We are not very accustomed to this dimension of the absence of ourselves.

If one is experiencing emotions such as joy, pity, sorrow, then has one created a subject-object relationship?

You must discriminate in you between what is emotion and what is emotivity. Emotivity is a reaction; it means you have established a personal relationship with a given moment. But in emotion, there's no subject-object relationship. In loving, love and being in love, there's no subject-object relationship. When you objectify joy, it is a form of mutilation, or, in other words, at the moment of being really happy you never say, "I am happy."

You can only be your presence; you can never know your presence. It is only in your total absence that you can be your presence. Don't take this as an intellectual formulation; go with it, feel what it means—your absence.

Could you say more about that moment when the subject-object relationship reappears?

Subject-object is mind, is memory. When you take yourself for a subject, you will see an object. An object without a subject doesn't exist. When there is no subject, there is no object. It is a bad habit to objectify yourself. Each time the reflex comes up, be aware of it. Think about it. I stop here.

How can you free yourself from memory?

When you really see the illusion of the "I," the "me," then you are free from memory. We speak of that memory which gives the "I," the "me," its existence. All memory used to build up security for maintaining the "I," the "me," is psychological. With the disappearance of the "I," the "me," psychological memory disappears and you are living in your presence. But as long as you live with the "I," the "me," you are not living in the present, you are either in the past or the future. You should become aware of this pendulum movement, past-future, past-future. It is the result of living constantly in end-gaining and anticipation: the becoming process. So see how you function, how you are completely detached from reality, how you live only past moments. Daydreaming and anticipation take so much energy, they waste all your creativity because there's only repetition. In life there is never repetition, every moment is new. It is the "I," the "me," which projects the already known, for the "I" can find no existence in the unknown. Seeing this whole mechanism is an instantaneous occurrence. What is the impact of this seeing on you? Don't let the seeing remain intellectual. What is the impact?

You tell us that in seeing the situation, the situation goes away, but I see that I don't really see the situation. How can I really see the situation?

When you meet someone, first see who meets the person; is it according to the position you have adopted? If you take the position of a woman, you will only see a man, but when you see somebody from the point of view of consciousness, from your totality, from your absence, then you see also the absence of the other. That is the real meeting, it is a meeting in love. But when you see the other from the point of view of a woman, then you are in conflict because all your way of speaking, all your way of seeing, all your way of appearing, is related to the woman. Then, after the meeting, you will see that you have perhaps not acted in quite the right way on the level of human relationships, free from any representation as a woman. You will see that the relationship in this moment was from object to object and that you were looking for security, to be loved, to be recognized, to be admired for your charm and so on. As you have very much charm, you produce all your charm, and in a certain way, why not? But the real charm appears when you are completely free from yourself; that charm is spontaneous, the other charm is a little contrived.

Dr. Klein, there seems to be a paradox, because the ego wants peace and joy and happiness, but it cannot have it without its own death. Can you say how one can reconcile this paradox?

The ego fears insecurity, the absence of happiness and of peace, and it looks from left to right in its search for happiness and peace. It explores many directions. Sometimes it meets situations where there was happiness, for example, when a desired object has been attained. But the ego did not notice that, at the moment of attainment, it was absent and there was happiness. It was an absolutely causeless moment. Because the ego was ignorant of this, it later said, "I had a beautiful moment because I met this or that person," or, "because I received this or that object." So look in all directions, and you will see that you can never find happiness in any direction or experience. In looking so, in all directions, there is a maturity that comes into your life, a faculty of higher reasoning, of higher understanding. You will stop looking in the objective world for

25

happiness. When you look in all directions and you can't find what you are looking for, there's a stop. This moment when you say, "I don't know," is crucial. In this moment all the energy which was projected in an eccentric direction comes back in a concentric way, and then comes to a total stop. In this total stop there's the "I am," but before the "I am" there must first be the "I don't know," the absence of all projection; for in this "I don't know," the "me," the "I" has no existence. But it is very important that you live with the "I don't know." It is in the real *living* "I don't know" that you know. When you say, "I don't know," you are completely open, free from all projections, free from all possible knowing.

Even though we say, "I don't know," we still try all kinds of practices. Then we get tired of them, don't want them any more and feel depressed.

But it's only an object that can be depressed. Your "I don't know" is still intellectual. You must really understand what it means to live completely in not-knowing. In this "I don't know" you feel your vastness, immensity, a kind of space without a frontier, without a center, you are nowhere. When you say, "I don't know," you will see that the looker is what he is looking for. When you look for the "I am" through techniques and systems, you objectify it. You must really see in your daily life that when you look for it, you go further away. When you see this, then there's a complete giving-up. There's a beautiful word in German, *gelassenheit*, a complete giving-up.

When you have something dirty, you need turpentine to remove it, so is it not good to have a sort of turpentine to transform your attachments?

But the mind can never change the mind. The mind doesn't know what is beyond the mind. When there's a stop of all possible mind, then it happens. You know how it is when you lose your key and you have looked everywhere, in every corner and in all the secret places, under, over, behind. What happens in your mind at this moment? It is completely free because there is no other possible direction to explore, there's no other place where the key could be.

A free mind is not "my" mind, and in this total absence you will feel your presence. As Sri Atmananda Krishna Menon said: "You will feel it without feeling it."

So do I have to be desperate before I am able to know "I don't know"?

Yes, you must come to a state of complete bankruptcy. Or more than bankruptcy, because often when there's bankruptcy there is still the idea that I could build up a new business! All possibilities must be completely abolished!

Is consciousness the only reality?

Consciousness is the only reality.

But in psychology they divide consciousness into subconscious and superconscious; is that just a trick of the mind?

Yes, a trick of the mind. There is only consciousness. Consciousness expresses itself in objects. When you see that every object flows out from consciousness, then there are no more "objects," there is only consciousness. The object loses its objectivity the moment it refers to consciousness.

But the collective consciousness of Gustav Jung, is that also the same, or is it an invention of Jung?

There is only consciousness, there is no division, there is no fraction. In this consciousness different qualities appear, but these qualities are different only in proportion. Just as there is no difference between the black body, the white, the yellow, the red. On the physical plane it is the same body, the same lungs, the same liver, the same hate, the same love, the same jealousy, the same fear, everywhere. It is only a question of proportion. There's no distinction. Looking for distinction is only trade by the mind. Looking for all this division is only the survival for the "me," the "I." When you discover that the "me" is an illusion, all psychology goes in the lake.

I HAVE A QUESTION *about pain in my upper back. I would like to sit in the way you tell us to sit but I can't do so because there are spasms in my back. If I try to let go it gets worse. What am I to do?*

That is a medical question. You must ask for a private meeting with me.

Dr. Klein, you have spoken about not having to do anything; however, you have also spoken about a certain maturity that is required. Are there systems or techniques to reach this maturity?

Look at your motives from day to day. Why are you projecting? Why are you expecting? See things around you as facts. In seeing the facts around you, you are not psychologically involved in them. Seeing things around you as facts frees you from psychological memory; it is a choiceless, selectionless looking. To behave in this way, you don't need any technique or system. In looking around you in this way, there is a ripening. When you take your surroundings as facts, you are completely detached from them; and spontaneous, appropriate action, which is not a reaction, may come up. You will see that these facts are in your awareness, in your autonomy. I think this is a moment when there is already a glimpse, a fore-feeling, of what we can say you are, your homeground, your basic nature. Because this innocent looking at the facts refers to itself. And there may be a moment when spontaneously the question comes up: "Who am I in all these surroundings?" Live with this question. You can be sure the question is the answer. But you have it in your hand, you can do it already, now, or do it tomorrow; have a good sleep and begin tomorrow!

Seeing the facts around you means you completely accept them. It is not a psychological, fatalistic acceptance, it is a functional acceptance. If you don't like the word accepting, then I would say welcome them; welcoming your surroundings gives your surroundings the dynamism to unfold. There's nobody who changes your life, it is only in really seeing the facts that change occurs. But this is no ordinary changing, it is really a transmutation of your surroundings. There may also be born some moments when you don't see any facts at all in your life, when there are gaps in which you feel freedom and happiness. Give it a very little place in your mind but don't think about it. It is important that there is understanding and that the understanding dissolves in being the understanding. Being the understanding is silent presence.

I would ask you what can be the meaning of a persistent pain in my solar plexus?

You must ask for some appointment. Why constantly bring these talks down to the earth?

What about the consciousness of people who are mentally handicapped?

You must love them.

Sometimes, it seems that my surroundings are choosing me and at other times it is me who makes the decisions. How can I get a balance between these two?

You can never make a decision. A decision which comes from you causes pain every time.

Do you mean to say that when one feels one has to make a decision, we should not make it?

30

When you see the facts, there is action; this action comes from the facts themselves.

During my listening to music, there's nothing but hearing, listening . . .

There's nobody who hears; there's only hearing.

And is not that the pure joy?

That is not the pure joy. The pure joy is after you have heard the whole music. The joy of seeing a play of Shakespeare, the real joy, is after the play.

Yes, I agree, but during the play or concert, I also enjoy myself.

Yes, because music is, in a certain way, sense perception, so there's some pleasure in it. Sounds produce some sensation in you.

That joy that comes afterwards is not an intellectual joy?

No, no. When you hear a Beethoven quartet today, the real joy may come tomorrow morning before you have completely woken up! Really, what I mean by joy is a kind of felicity.

When I have thoughts, it is not so difficult to see them and to take a little distance from them, but my feelings overwhelm me and I have difficulty in objectifying them. I am emotionally involved more with feelings than with thoughts, especially with unpleasant feelings.

If it's an unpleasant feeling, then it does not give you any security, so you call it fear. The first thing is to free yourself from the concept fear, because the concept fear is memory. The concept has nothing to do with the actual fear, the fear in the moment itself. So let go of the concept fear and face the actual perception. Make a really pure perception of your fear, let it completely unfold, feel it in your body. In a certain way it is compressed energy that frees itself as it unfolds. And it can only unfold when there's no longer any "I" to be an accomplice to it and when there is an innocent accepting, an innocent listening, innocent seeing. But you can only understand this in experiencing the pure perception. You are not accustomed

31

to pure perception, because you immediately judge, compare, interpret, justify and so on. The percept is real, but the concept is only memory. The concept comes in very quickly.

Sometimes it occurs to me that, when listening to you, I am not conscious of having a body and even your voice doesn't seem to come from outside, from another person, but it is a voice that is in myself, in my space. What I wanted to ask you was: Does it mean that I am in the listening you are talking about?

Absolutely.

Then the question is, how to use it in daily life?

You have the model here, so transpose it into daily life, for example, with your boyfriend. It should not be a problem!

Could it be that sometimes I think I understand what you are saying and at other times I don't understand at all?

It is very good that you never understand it!

But I want to understand you.

But *feel* the understanding. When you say you cannot understand, it means you cannot concretize it. Have you ever met a person and after the meeting you have a very lovely feeling where there's no reasoning, there's no thinking, there's only a love feeling?

For discovering your real nature, is it necessary to have personal contact with a teacher?

That is why I come here.

And the teacher is realized?

First be clear about the notion of a teacher. Teaching occurs when there is no teacher. On the level of a teacher, it means somebody apparently knows and somebody does not know. In this relationship no teaching is possible. Teaching is when there is no teacher and when there is no pupil. The teacher does not give any hold to the pupil to be a pupil. Then there is a real relation.

That means then that the teacher and the pupil are one, but at this moment I don't feel this.

That is because you take yourself for an ignorant man.

How can I not take myself for ignorant when I am? (laughter)

How can you free yourself from this ignorance? That is your real question. Just free yourself from the idea that you are ignorant; and to free yourself from this idea, you must simply listen. Find that listening moment in yourself, that moment when you completely give up; find the not-knowing moment. When you have given up, you are totally open, as open as when you are caught by surprise or astonishment.

In the spiritual books they sometimes say that the guru knows exactly where the disciple is as far as the spiritual level is concerned, but if the guru has a picture of a disciple at a specific time in the sadhana, does it not bind the disciple to an image?

The guru knows quite well the level of the disciple; he waits only for the moment when the disciple sees clearly that he is nothing-ness. This moment of complete openness, innocence, is the oppor-tunity, the open window through which the light, the flame of the guru, transmits a flame to the disciple. The transmission of the flame is not intentional. It happens spontaneously when openness meets itself.

In this kind of meeting the answer belongs to the person asking the question, but everyone present must transpose the answer to their own questions, their own moments in life.

How can I best hear your answer?

Do not immediately find a conclusion or interpretation. When the words are grasped by the mind, the mind puts them in the freezer for later consumption. But this food from the guru is spoiled in the freezer, it becomes dead food. So listen without finding a solution in the moment itself. Let it remain in non-understanding; let it remain in not-knowing. When you live completely in not-knowing, then one day it becomes knowing. That is why you must live with the question. The mind can never find the answer; it is the mind that hinders the answer, because the living answer is beyond the mind. So, coming back to the question of maturity, when there's maturity, many questions come up in your life but you don't make any effort to find the solution to the question which comes to you. Rather, you live with the question as you'd live with a bird in your hand: when you put pressure on it, it dies.

If you see a baby just after being born it is open but gradually it develops an ego. My question is: Is it not necessary to have a strongly developed ego just in order to be able to drop it?

It is an idea of Aurobindo. When the child is in the womb of the mother, it already appropriates itself to this surrounding. All that the mother absorbs, thinks and feels is food for the baby. Then in nine months, the apparently born child appropriates itself in its other surroundings. It is the beginning of biological survival. It is only later that the child says, "I want." It depends on the father and mother and the nearest surroundings as to how to give security to the child without forming an ego. You must ignore the ego, you don't especially need to see it to free yourself from it.

Is it possible to perceive people like any other facts?

Yes. Seeing facts is a love relationship with your surroundings. When you meet somebody you are completely open, there's no reflex to immediately interpret. Generally you think, "He has a big forehead, long ears, a big nose, he is clever or nice," and so on. In seeing only the facts, you don't judge at all; you are open to him, all your five senses are open, your whole body is open to meet him. In this way you give the opportunity to the person you meet to be completely free, because you don't superimpose on him any knowledge that you know already. In postponing all qualification, you meet the person in your freedom from qualifications and you help create an unqualified person through your way of approaching him. Then it is a beautiful meeting, because it is not a relation of object to object. When you find yourself knowingly in your absence, you stimulate this absence in the other. This is the most human way to meet, because then when you meet somebody, you meet yourself. Whom can you meet? Whom? There's not a "you" and an "other."

If I don't understand what you say, is it because I am not ripe?

Wait till it becomes understanding in you, but don't keep the understanding in the garage of the mind. The understanding must dissolve in being the understanding, in silent awareness, otherwise it remains only representation. When there is real understanding, what has not been understood dissolves in being understanding.

When one is walking in nature and it feels as though nature is inside oneself, is that an example of the dissolving of the ego?

When you walk in the forest, there's not a walker; there's only walking. You are surrounded by trees but you don't qualify them, you don't name them, you remain in direct perception. You are nowhere, you are not localized; your mind is completely free from any representation. Then you really have a love relation with your surroundings. You can say then that you live in a "thanking feeling" with your surroundings, because nature around you is waiting for thankfulness. It is nature that helps you to be a human being and you help also the surroundings to be what they are. When you are in this state that you described, nature is waiting for your thankfulness .

If you see nature and other people around you as facts, does every meeting have the same basic coloring?

Yes, love has the same coloring.
    Thank you.

*W*E WOULD LIKE TO BE SPIRITUAL *and because we want it so very much, we try everything. How can we know that we are on the right path? We can be distracted onto a false way so how can we know we have chosen the right path?*

I ask you: Are you happy? It is the unhappiness in you that looks for something. There is in you a lack. You have already looked in many directions but still there's a lack of freedom. If you really understand this and follow this understanding, automatically there's a stop to all looking. Be completely attuned to this stopping moment; it opens you to a new direction, a dimension of not-knowing. You are awake in this dimension of not-knowing. But you come only to this moment when you have looked in many directions.

Why do we meditate?

We don't meditate. We sit quietly and we enjoy being together. There's only stillness, there's nobody to be still here. Stillness is our fundamental nature. In stillness you are not separate, you are one.

When you said yesterday that there is only one lung, one liver, etc., did you mean that every human being has precisely the same experience of what it is to live in a body?

There's nothing special, there's not an independent entity. The body with the white skin, yellow skin, black skin, is the same body, with the same organs. A black man's organs can perfectly operate in a white man, there's no difference. The hate that you find in a white man is the same hate as you find in a black, red or yellow man. The black man is as jealous as the white man. So what are you looking for that's special?

I'm just wanting to understand properly what you said; it's the first time that I've heard you say that about the physical body, although you've said it many times about sorrow and hatred.

There's no difference in human beings; differences are only in your mind. Are you looking for an individual entity which you think would be a little more romantic?

Is the mind always split?

As long as there's a split mind you live in bondage. So the best is to accustom yourself, to familiarize yourself, with choiceless observation. You will one day find yourself in this awareness without selection.

Are our observations and our emotions illusions?

It depends from which point of view you look at it. When you deeply look into things you will see that what you look at is in the looker. The looked-at has no existence in itself; it exists through the looker. It has its potentiality in the looker, for there are not two, there is only one.

So you could say if there is no looker, the looking also disappears?

No, there is *only* looking; that is your original nature.

OK.

Not so quick! What does this word OK refer to?

38

Don't we all have our individual ways that are different, our particular ways?

Yes, but we put all into categories. When a man now meets a woman he says, "What is your sign? Are you a Scorpio or a Leo?" That's categorizing the woman into two signs out of twelve!

I'm coming back to the black and white people and I was a little astonished when I saw your latest book had Plato quoted in the preface. Wasn't it just Plato who divided things into a higher and a lower world, who placed them on different levels?

He spoke of the transcendent and the immanent, but that is only a division of the mind. Where does the transcendent begin and where does the immanent begin? It doesn't exist in reality. It is very beautiful when Plato says that one must live with the question, one must love his own question and not try to interpret through the already known. The answer is in the instantaneous appearing.

You spoke yesterday about the use of higher reason. Can you say what that is and also what ordinary reason is?

Taking your expression, "ordinary reason," this is when you deal with objects. But when you deal with something which is object-less, not an object, there appears another quality of reasoning. When reasoning concerns mathematics or geometry, etc., we call it ordinary reason. But when you deal with something which is completely objectless it brings you to a new way of looking at things. Very often the answers here belong to higher reason. In a certain way you ask the question and the question is heard in silence, and I would say the answer also comes out of silence—what we call in Sanskrit *vidyavritti*.

How can we be sure that the longing for realization or truth is not still the ego seeking security?

You can only be the truth, you can never know the truth. This knowing is heard in the absence of yourself, when there is no

39

representation; then there is a certitude. Truth brings its own certitude; it needs no proof, it is its own proof. All that appears around you could be doubtful, but the nearest—that means consciousness—can never belong to doubt. All that you think you can look for belongs to the already known. But peace, happiness, love and joy can never be put in the frame of the known, that is, time and space. Your first experience of peace may be through the experience of deep sleep. It is deep sleep which awakens the desire to be peace also in the waking state. When the body wakes up in the morning there's a residue of this experience that you had in deep sleep. So you desire something that you profoundly know already.

There are moments in daily life when there is a natural giving-up of things. You don't make any effort to give up, but things simply have no more reason to be. When you have a taste of these moments, don't escape them, be completely attuned to them. Don't mistake them for an absence; in this absence is your presence.

Would you say that our breath balances between the known and the unknown?

Yes, yes. The moment when the exhalation is completely accomplished is not an absence of breathing. You touch the ultimate reality in this moment. Exhalation and inhalation are superimposed on reality. The picture changes every day, but the background on which the picture appears, never changes. So, be this background knowingly; don't take it for an absence of breathing. In the exhalation you die; it is a natural giving-up. There's no person who gives up; there's just giving-up.

You can only discover what you already know. You may say, "I have found something new," but there's nothing new; it is only the old which has a new package. You can divide all that is objective, all that is perceived into a thousand pieces, like a scientist. You can put it in two thousand pieces and you can put it into more than two thousand pieces but, as Oppenheimer said, you can never find the perceiver through any amount of analysis, because we *are* the perceiving. What we are we can never perceive, we can only be.

In the context of your last answer, where is the possibility to be creative?

When you are open to the unknown, there's no more repetition; then there's creativity. In creativity objects are expressions of admiring, of thanking to be. Producing art, poetry, is an act of giving, offering, for there is nobody to offer anything, there's only the love of offering, and this gesture of offering comes from the unknown, from silence, comes out of thanking to be. This I understand to be creativity, otherwise there is only a manipulation of the already known. That is the difference between a work of art and an artistic production.

What is it that transforms occasional moments of clarity into a continuous condition?

It is only in your openness that you are available to truth. When you once have the glimpse of this intuition, you will also have it another time, because the mind now knows that what it wants is beyond it. The mind is now open to what is beyond the mind, so truth will solicit you quite often. Before going to sleep you will find yourself easily giving up what you are not. Then you live in your own nakedness. You will also feel it before the body wakes up in the morning and when the thinking process is over. These moments are not the absence of thinking or action, but the same truth. Truth is waiting constantly for its establishment.

Now you are open to the new dimension. The first glimpse is a window in the darkness. Through this window, light flows in; light which comes through this window is not the pure absolute light, but it is an expression of this light. But if you will once follow this light, then you will come out of the window to where truth is established—neither outside nor inside. The first glimpse is necessary.

So, as you now know that there is some reality beyond the thinking process, you will automatically be open to these moments; it is enough that the thought process is finished

But you can never go to it, because in trying to go to it you go away from it; the seeker is the sought.

That means you can never help another person in his search?

By being in truth you are already helping. Being in truth is automatically helping. There is no helper. Your presence alone helps. Your presence is stimulating, you stimulate your surroundings when you live spontaneously the stimulating; don't try to stimulate anyone or anything.

*I*S THIS THE APPROPRIATE MOMENT *to ask you a medical question?*

I don't think so, but try.

It concerns an illness. Should one always consider illness as a disharmony in the brain, in thinking and feeling, or could it be something concerning the immune system of the body?

Take the perception as a fact, but don't try to interpret it.

What is happening when the body shakes vigorously and heavily during meditation?

Go with the shaking. When you refuse it, then you feed it and it will be exaggerated. There is an inner rhythm in the body which brings you to a kind of freedom from nervosity. You know there are certain rituals in the Jewish tradition and in the Mohammedan, and so on, where movement plays a role. This organic movement brings you to a certain tranquility.

You said yesterday to look at our surroundings and what is happening as facts, and not be involved emotionally. My question is, if the things that are happening are so close that it is difficult to take a distance, what can one do?

The observing of your environment begins with your body, your resistance, your agitation, compensation and so on—all that appears. Become acquainted, look at your surroundings with a fresh observation, without interpretation. When you see your surroundings from a point of view there is very often conflict, because a point of view is a fraction and a fraction can only see fractions. So any action which flows out of this fraction is a fractional action. When you see the situation from your wholeness, from your completeness, you will see many things you did not see before. These things make the situation completely clear. It brings instant choice without choosing.

If you are living constantly in openness, is it the way to enlightenment, or is it already enlightenment?

When there is total understanding that the personal entity is an illusion, one could say at this moment there is enlightenment, because there is nobody to be enlightened.

During this week we have done body-work in the mornings and in the afternoons we try more or less to reach that spiritual understanding. What is the connection between the two?

Why put all these activities into categories?

I should like to abolish the idea of categories; therefore, I would like to see the connection.

In the morning and in the afternoon and even in the night, everywhere and at every moment, we emphasize presence, we emphasize looking. In the morning we say it's our body and in the afternoon we say it's our mind. You are looking for clarity, but you can see in the morning that there is absolutely no clarity in the body.

I have the impression that my morning work is not perfect yet.

You judge it; better not to worry. Don't put the expressions of life into categories. Daily life calls for a certain number of positions, so you function, you make connections with what life asks of you.

When you really listen to your daily occupation, you will function simply. There are many functions: when you are with your husband, your boyfriend, when you wash the dishes, when you teach. What is important is that you don't establish a personal relationship with your doings, as you know there is no doer.

So during the body-work we should not at all have the idea that "I" have to put my arm in the vertical position, but it should be more letting-go, like a stream.

You give an order to your body and your body executes the movement. But don't remain in the residue of the order. Live completely in the perception, with the feeling.

Now I see that I am not quite in the right mood when I am doing the body-work.

You cannot at the same time give an order and execute the order.

But while I am doing what my brain told me to do, there's something, which I think is my intellectual part, that is following what is happening.

The body takes itself in charge, executes an order when you give it; it lives in your attention, in your presence, free from any projections to attain or achieve. Look at your body as you would look at a child playing, a bird flying; simply function. When your body asks for food, you take food; when you are thirsty, you drink. Don't make a problem of drinking water.

Sometimes I have the feeling that I am quite open and that I am living in that openness, but at the same time I have the feeling that my body doesn't understand.

In this openness the body is also open. In this openness there is only giving.

Sometimes it seems impossible for the body to let go, to give.

Don't judge yourself at this moment. Take note of it. When you go away from your openness you will feel yourself in the dark; see it, that is enough. This seeing is not from the mind, because the mind interprets, judges, compares, justifies. Just take note. In other words, be aware of such moments; then you will live this openness very often, you will be integrated completely. It is only in this openness that you are a lovely being.

But is it possible that even while being that lovable being your body can feel pain?

Take it also as it comes. When you accept it, when you see it, you will find some solution.

Last year you spoke about listening and this year again you speak about listening. I think it is very important to listen, but I experience it as very difficult.

Don't use the word difficult; use another word. Difficult doesn't exist.

When I am open, I see that for a while I am in listening, then it stops because an emotional fear comes up. What am I to do in that moment?

Understand first the quality of listening. I use the word quality, but in reality listening is quality-less; there's no quality in listening, there's only listening. In this non-quality of listening, understanding really, there's no listener. In listening there is no concentrating, no fixation.

If I really understand you, there's no cause and effect. When I look at my environment I see it as the result of my actions.

When you think of the cause, there is no effect; when you think of the effect, there is no cause. Cause and effect is memory, like subject and object.

What do you call a cause? There are so many causes. What was the cause of the last war? Can we find the causes? In daily life it is very difficult to go away from cause and effect, it is true, but when speaking in this kind of meeting, one cause may have very many other causes. You are the result of your father and mother and your father and mother are the result of their father and mother, too, so where are the causes?

If you are in openness, could you say that your body is serving that presence?

Yes. The body is a vehicle with which you must not identify yourself. Your knowledge, your personality, is a vehicle, you use it; but to identify yourself with your personality is a restriction. The body is an instrument which it is necessary to maintain well.

So when you are in openness you might say something you didn't first think about, you didn't first work out in your mind?

You will have an intuition in a certain moment, and this intuition calls for a certain type of action in the world of space and time.

You spoke of a certain maturity that comes after having explored many different directions. I was a very young man when I met you. So my question is: Should I just go on and look into psychoanalysis, astrology or something? Just to make sure that it doesn't really mean anything?

You know certain feelings which belong to the relationship with your mother, you know them very well. Become more and more acquainted with these feelings, with this identification. See your mother as a friend, not as a mother. Your mother sees you as her son, but don't give any hold to it. Your mother is extremely intelligent, and understands both what a relationship between mother and son means and what a relationship means where there is no "mother" and "son" relation. There is an old reflex to take yourself as a son, but when you see your mother really as a friend, I think very soon you will be free from this identification. Psychiatrists will take your money, so don't spend it on these kinds of things.

This morning there was an unpleasant situation at work. I tried to see it from my openness but it didn't work. This morning I couldn't have the outlook that was necessary and now as I sit here I see the situation and I can laugh. Would that mean that being outside work is a good apprenticeship for me?

The moment you feel a situation as unpleasant, don't try to interpret or overcome or in any way manipulate it. Feel only the effect in your body; the effect is very deep-rooted. To free yourself from the effect, feel the perception—it will unfold in your looking. Once you are free from the perception, you will see the whole situation from this impersonal point of view and you will really laugh.

If in the situation as described in this moment there is a feeling of guilt, could we use that feeling in a positive way?

Who feels guilty? You will not find the entity. That frees you from the state of feeling guilty. Talking in religious terms, I would say there is forgiving. But as long as you believe yourself to be an independent entity, you cannot free yourself from guilt.

Did I understand you rightly when you said there are moments when the personality will come and go when you need it? And would this mean that there are moments when you need the personality?

When the person is seen as an illusion, then everything for maintaining the person disappears and nothing remains that is personal. What remains is universal, plastic, not fixed; it appears spontaneously when you need it and disappears when the moment is over. It is a vehicle that appears in your awareness; there is no identification with it.

If you encounter or perceive a situation which society would normally judge to be morally unsound, how would you deal with it?

When you are not the doer and there is only doing, the situation belongs to your awareness. Action is according to your awareness, it doesn't go through the mind. But the moment you identify yourself with the doer, it becomes a problem. As long as you take yourself for a person, you are responsible. When you are free from the person, the question of whether or not you are responsible doesn't come up, because you are adequate, appropriate to every situation. What is important is to wake up in the total absence of oneself; in this total absence there is really presence. You should first understand it and explore it.

There are many questions. Let us continue tomorrow.

I S ONE ALONE *when living in openness?*

In openness there is nobody, so the question of being alone doesn't arise. But don't *try* to be open, because openness is your real nature; it is the eternal waiting without waiting. When you sit here without purpose, spontaneously you are open. Openness refers to itself.

Could you say that openness is like a mirror in which things appear and disappear and from which actions spontaneously occur?

In openness action appears spontaneously, because it is free from intention; the goal is attained from moment to moment. But you try to make a state of openness. Be aware when you try to be open. See how you make being open, being silent, a purpose.

Can I ask about the music we heard last night? I didn't understand why there was no applause after the playing.

Because it is barbaric to make that noise! There's nobody who plays, there's only playing. You make this noise for whom? When the sound lives and dies in your silence, that barbaric applause is a violence on your whole psychosomatic structure.

I am inspired by applause and on the other hand the public in the auditorium is stimulated by it, the tension is lowered.

If you must clap, at least wait until all the sounds have died away and you feel them dissolve in your silence. But the question doesn't really belong here.

Thank you very much.

I have a question which arises out of something you said during the body-work this morning. If I understood you correctly, you said that you felt that neither jogging nor cycling were particularly beneficial, because they were generally both done with anticipation. My question is twofold: Firstly, do you feel that it is possible to carry out these activities without anticipation?

Of course.

If it is possible to do these activities without anticipation, then do you feel that they are beneficial at more than merely the physical level?

It is for the joy of doing it in the moment itself. You do many things in your life without profit, only for the joy of seeing it, the joy of doing it.

That is the point I am making. I have had much joy out of jogging, simply without having any relationship with the activity, and so I don't understand what it was you said that was not beneficial about jogging and cycling?

There is nothing beneficial, there is only the love of doing it. Don't look for any return; do something because you love it. What you have learned here, you must transpose to your cycling and your jogging and your other activities. In doing it the right way there will be joy.

Sometimes in meditation I have the feeling that every sound around seems to be within me; but sometimes it is so sharp and painful and I feel it like a vibration in different places in my body. I ask myself what does it mean and what is it?

Nothing is outside. All is in you. It is you who project it, and it comes back to you. It has all its reality in you; welcome it completely. When you really welcome, there is no pain. In the converging of pain and joy, there is real joy. That joy is not relative, the other joy is still relative because it is the contrary of pain.

Yesterday you told us that we are too much in the head, too much here in front, and that we should try to be more in the back of the head. I tried to do that, but then I feel that I am no longer in meditation because I am now trying to do something.

The first thing is to be free from the factory of producing thoughts, which is in the frontal region. You can never fight your thoughts. In fighting them, you feed them, so free yourself from this factory and localize yourself temporarily behind your head, more or less in the small brain in the seventh cervical where the energy is condensed. Then you will see how your brain is completely relaxed, free, open. This localization behind is only temporary. Sooner or later it goes down to your heart. Your heart is the last door, and when you go out of this door you are nowhere, neither inside nor outside. But don't make a technique of it.

How can I not make a technique of it?

Experience it several times; then you will see how it is a natural, I would say, an organic, feeling of relaxation. Then you will come spontaneously to live it, because you have seen another quality of your brain. But generally, when you direct your attention to some muscle function, in a certain way you feed it. So don't face it straight on, ignore it. I mention this occasionally. You should not emphasize it; it is a secret for you, don't forget it!

When you spoke of openness you said not to make a state of it. Does that mean that you should simply live it and not comment on it or make any mental movement?

Sitting here is without any purpose. Contemplate profoundly what it means: being without purpose. Feel also what the word purposeless means for you; it has a strong impact. When you think of station, when you think of chair or carpet, it has not a strong impact on you, but when you speak of love, when you speak of purposelessness, being without intention, the impact is tremendous, because your real nature is purposeless. When there is no goal the goal is attained. So discover, explore totally what it means for you to be without purpose, to be free from everything. But when you come here and make a state of it, that is not meditation. When you come here, take it as a laboratory. It is a laboratory only to see that there is not a meditator, for you cannot find the meditator. As long as you think there's a meditator, you "do" it constantly, you "meditate." The meditator is only a representation of your brain, it is a figment in your mind. When you think there is something to meditate on, you only meditate on what you know already, so you turn in a vicious circle. In reality meditation is from moment to moment, it is your background, it is the light behind all perceptions. It gives life to all perceptions, it gives reality to all that is perceived. You can never understand what meditation is, or what God is, what love is, what peace or freedom is; it is beyond the mind. I think it is important that you don't just take for granted what I say to you. When it comes to you, think it over and it will bring you to understanding and the giving up of anticipation and daydreaming. There are so many timeless moments when you are spontaneously in meditation, when you are free from planning, strategies and daydreaming, you will discover that you are very often in your purposelessness. You will discover the jewel I offer to you. Take it.

(long pause)

Since the beginning of this seminar, I am a little divided in my thinking, because I feel I have the need to ask a question and at the same time I say to myself: Don't ask a question, find out for yourself.

There is a spontaneous question that comes not from book knowledge or from hearsay. It is a real question. When it comes up, you will not refuse it.

It is a question coming from experience.

Of course, all that is not experience has no meaning.

The more I have the intention to give up things in which I am interested, especially yoga, meditation, because what happens is that I try to become someone . . .

First formulate clearly for yourself what you want to say. Formulating it brings clarity. But when you are not clear you cannot formulate it. So, make it clear to yourself; then you can formulate it. Now what is your question?

That I want to give up all yoga and meditation and live an ordinary life without any kind of spiritual exercises. But when I do that, I feel no satisfaction, so I feel trapped.

Who would like to live an ordinary life? Find out who it is. Next year, when you have the chance to come back again, you can tell me who it is.

Is ignorance ignorance of reality or of illusion?

There is only reality. But what is not understood in relation to this reality is ignorance. The moment when what you call ignorance refers to reality, then it is true. So when you take yourself for somebody, for a personal entity, you contact your surroundings with this personality, you live in a dream, you live in an illusion. But the moment you have understood that what you call yourself is nothing other than an object, then you look at your surroundings from your completeness and your wholeness, and all that is around you, that you do or think, is creative. You are really creative in your absence. Think it out, what it means: absence. See how it acts on you when you think about it, that you *are* in your absence, free from all representation. You will have the opportunity before going to sleep at night to think about it, and then you will be free from thinking.

55

*I*S DAYDREAMING AN EXPRESSION *of the residue of judging, comparison, choice, etc.?*

It is the "I," the "me," that is looking for survival in two ways: in projecting a future, or going back to the past for enjoyment. It is an enormous waste of energy. Don't try not to do it, but see the moment the reflex comes up.

What do you mean by reflex?

There is a moment when you are aware that you are daydreaming. In this moment when you are aware, there is no daydreaming. Sustain this stopping moment, neither refuse nor indulge thoughts. Simply feel yourself in the stopping. Feel the impact of being in the stopping, in the taking-note. After you have taken note several times that you have been daydreaming, there's a moment you will become aware as soon as the impulse comes up, before the formulation into a representation. In other words, you will find yourself first after the daydreaming, then during, then before. But take note of it. It is not a mental taking note, but see how it acts on you, feel the impact.

Understanding and living your words has changed my way of living at home. I notice my surroundings are changing as well, since those sur-

roundings belong to me. But a difficulty arises when someone, especially someone close, won't accept the way I function.

It is only through silence that you can change your surroundings. When you need to formulate, to clarify thinking in words, you must wait for the right opportunity. It must be the right moment if it is to act on your surroundings. It is often much more powerful when you keep it in silence.

When your surroundings take you for a person, for a daughter, for a wife, for a mother, you must not give any hold to them. Your position—not to identify yourself as a daughter, as a wife, as a mother—acts on your surroundings.

[Aside, to someone: Don't write. You cannot listen and write; leave it, please.]

It is you who makes your surroundings free, free from the image. Do you see what I mean? The mother, the wife, the daughter comes up from time to time, but it comes up in nothingness, in freedom from the I-image, in your total absence. That is really a love relation. There are moments when you need to be a mother, but you don't try to be a mother; you are a mother because it is life which asks you to be a mother. When your husband asks you to be a woman, you are a woman; you don't try to be a woman for your husband—it is in the moment itself. It is only in these circumstances, when you are completely free from the concept "woman," that you are a real woman; otherwise you are not a real woman, it is artificial.

I'd like to ask you a question about one aspect of using the mind. You have said that there is only seeing and there is only listening, and when we go for a walk in the country there is just walking. It seems that the minute the mind starts to be used, a problem arises in that one becomes sucked into the thing that one is trying to work out. In other words the seeing, the listening, the walking seem sort of passive. How, for example, does one work out a difficult legal document?

In listening, in seeing, you are completely alert, lucid, clear-minded, with all your energy condensed, not dispersed, at your disposal. At the same time you are open to the circumstances. It is an active-passive state: you are active in your lucidity, in your presence, your awareness; and passive in not interfering with the mind, thoughts, judgment, comparison, and so on. In a certain way, you wait; it is only in waiting that there is unfolding. Yesterday you went to the museum and you were looking, I remember, at the paintings of Mondrian. When you look at the paintings as an artist, when you look as a poet, the object unfolds. The percept is rich; the concept, in a certain way, has no value. There is not a seer, there is not a looker, there is not a hearer, there is not a toucher; there is touching, there is hearing, there is listening.

You are looking, you are open to the unknown; but you use the tools, the instruments at your disposal to formulate the unknown. Creative thinking, creative doing, is completely different from how we generally think. There is a difference between rational, practical, calculative thinking, and creative thinking. Rational thinking, calculative thinking, starts with thinking, starts with thought. But creative thinking never starts with thought, it starts with silence. Practical thinking, rational thinking can have its homeground in silence, but generally when we use practical, rational thinking we start from thought. This kind of thinking can bring us to misery.

In practical life you must take facts as they are; don't start from knowledge, from psychological memory. First there is inquiring, watching, and then comes acting. So live in not-knowing, free from memory. Then perceptions are very rich. We are not accustomed enough to seeing things without memory. When you live with the pure perception without any mental interference, you see the whole history of what you are looking at. A kind of metamorphosis takes place. Things are always new. As we saw yesterday in the sculpture by Henry Moore, and the one by Lipchitz, the artist doesn't repeat what God has created.

I feel somehow that if I live without the person, there is a chance that I might become crazy.

Who, who can become crazy? There's something confused in you!

I have believed for a very long time that knowledge alone will lead to realization, and this is very difficult to give up.

With this knowledge you live in the known forever. The known can never bring you to the unknown. Knowledge must make you free from knowledge, and the question now is: How can knowledge make you free from knowledge? It means that the mind must come to an end; it must see its incompetence in the moment itself. When the mind sees its limits, there's a stopping of the mind function and knowledge vanishes in being knowledge. Then you live really in your total absence; you live in your vastness, your immensity, where there's no border and no center. In other words, you live in your total felicity. Knowledge can teach you to learn a language or a science, to use words for poetry, to learn how to play the piano, but when the question "Who am I?" comes up, then already a certain maturity has been attained, and at that point knowledge is no more use. You know from your own experience that there are moments when there's an absence of knowledge, but these moments are not a real absence, because that absence still refers to the possible presence of knowledge. So the real absence is after the absence, and the presence, logically speaking, must be a double absence. Then there is neither absence nor presence. Both dissolve in the "I am."

In the morning before the body is completely integrated, there are moments when there's no reference to anything, completely purposeless moments when there's no projection to become. These moments you know. Make yourself more and more acquainted with these moments. Become completely attuned to them without trying to know them. This knowing is beyond knowing, before knowledge. For you, I would say: What is the nearest? The nearest is not your body, not your senses, not your mind, because your nearest is before the mind, before the senses, before the body. It is not a way of thinking, it is a way of feeling; go completely in.

Would you say that many jobs in modern society prevent one from living in openness and so should be avoided?

You are in the society, but don't be the society. You function in this society, but don't think of yourself as an Englishman. Be nobody. When you are nobody, you live your fullness. Of course, it is very difficult not to be English! (laughter) But do not identify yourself with it.

Would you say that in openness there is only openness and therefore there can be no rejection?

All that appears around you, all that exists, belongs to you, has its potentiality in your openness; all refers to your openness, finds its meaningfulness in your openness. We have no personal relationship with our surroundings, because the person doesn't exist. The "person" reacts, the "person" resists. When there's reaction, you can say you have established a personal relationship with the object, with your surroundings.

In your openness all that appears refers to your openness; things are in your openness, but you are not in things, for you live totally your own autonomy. You live really your freedom and you make your surroundings free.

HAVE YOU ANYTHING TO SAY?

Can you tell us how it is, always to be in openness?

Don't try to be open, don't project; live from moment to moment. Feel deeply what it means: open. The word open is not the experience open. It is a symbol. So see how the symbol acts on you. It acts on the level of the senses. Be completely attuned to it, otherwise the word remains simply a concept. When you say, "I am open," it means that you are completely unfurnished, but on the level of the senses you are immensity.

Is it so that in a situation of openness, no memory remains?

In openness you are completely empty, receptive, welcoming; the welcoming is not polluted by the mind.

Can you tell us how to cope with memories?

See that what you think to be is also memory, and that you identify with it. To maintain it you need memory, so ignore it. You live your presence when you are really absent.

Does it make sense then to go into therapy, to know emotions and feelings?

It is meaningless, it is more or less to maintain the idea of being something. Discover yourself more and more in the space where there is a complete absence of yourself. That is real stillness. Inquiring brings you to the moment when you see really, live really, what you have been and what you will be, eternally. What you are fundamentally, you are it; it can never be an object. All that you try to obtain, to achieve, is an object. In all your achievements you can only find objects, but the subject can never be an object, can never be perceived because you are it. When all the striving energy comes to a stop, you will find yourself in this silent presence.

You have understood logically now that you can never be an object, that you can never find the subject. So give up looking and be it. Live this silent presence, don't try to make it objective; it is non-dual. That is why I said, practically speaking, go away from the factory that is producing concepts, and you will find yourself as if behind yourself. It is only when you are "behind" yourself that there can be some glimpse of what we are speaking about here.

In deep sleep there is the joy of being absent. So I ask: Why wake up?

When you say, "I'm awake," that means you are awake in objects; but in reality you are sleeping. To wake up in your real nature is the only meaning of being awake; everything else is only dreaming and sleeping. It is only the experience in deep sleep which brings you to ask yourself: What is life? It is the residue of this non-dual experience, which is still in our phenomenal body, which brings us to this question. You must live with this residue.

Should I think about everything that has been said, or not think about it at all?

First be completely open to the perfume. When you keep the scent, then you will be solicited by it. But when you keep only the formulation, the words, then you keep it in the garage. So what is important is to keep the flavor, otherwise you keep only the skin of the mango and not the flesh. Don't try to remember the words, but be totally open and you can be sure they will come to you.

ON MEDITATION

You will feel in your meditation that there is still a residue of the idea of finding something, but we have very often repeated that the seeker *is* the sought. What you are fundamentally you can never objectify because you *are* it. An object is a fraction; it appears in your wholeness, in your globality. When you really come to the understanding that the seeker is the sought, there is a natural giving-up of all energy to find something. It is an instantaneous apperception. I don't say perception, because in perception there is a perceiver and something perceived. An apperception is an instantaneous perceiving of what is perceiving. So it can never be in a relation of subject-object, just as an eye can never see its own seeing. That is why I said you will first find yourself behind yourself. I say behind yourself because you know yourself mainly in subject-object relationship, in your factory, in your forehead. The energy which strikes the factory in a certain moment and makes the factory work is localized behind, so stay with the energy behind and you will find a glimpse of non-subject-object relationship. This glimpse is seen with your whole intelligence which is there in the absence of the person, the thinker, the doer. Understanding, *being the understanding,* is enlightenment.

(silence)

You can never perceive your globality, your wholeness. If there is a perceiver, it is not your wholeness. Your globality, your wholeness, is its own perceiving. So it is clear your globality can never be perceived, it can never be an object. It is non-dual. It must be clear for the mind that what you are looking for is the looking itself. When you really see this with your intelligence and love and understanding, there is a natural giving-up of all projected energy. All energy directed towards finding something comes back to its

65

homeground. This moment of equilibrium, you must live. It is purposeless because it is what you fundamentally are.

In this non-dual non-state you cannot speak of relation. You must visualize this relationless state, you must love it, you must approach it with your whole intelligence. This is the only thing that you should remember; everything else that has been said can be put in the waste basket!

San Rafael, California

February 1989

Beautiful trees, the scent of eucalyptus and pine in the cold air. We came from all over the world and shared the intimacy of living in close quarters around the central courtyard of the Santa Sabina Center. One day there were pebble-sized hailstones and we shivered as we explored together all the ways of looking for survival: anger, frustration, fear, attraction, fixed ideas, unnecessary chatter, jealousy, tension in the body. In this adventure one must keep one's center. In the light of whole seeing, all fractions dissolve in love.

T HIS WEEK IS FOR FINDING OUT TOGETHER what we are fundamentally, our real nature. Finding out, inquiring, needs an attention free from all expectation and anticipation, I would say, an innocent attention. We can never find out what we are; we can only find out what we are not, because we are, in any case what we are. To know what we are not we must discover what it is that we are not: our body-mind.

We have not really a fixed program, but in the morning is a quiet sitting. It is meditation without a meditator and without something meditated on. It is our natural stillness. Later in the morning we will explore our body, its tension, fear, anxiety, aggression; and the mental understanding is in the afternoon. The teaching is based primarily on understanding, or, I would say, *being* understanding. Understanding is the result of right observation. It is a welcoming observation without judgement, comparison or interpretation. It is simply observing. We cannot objectify it. We cannot localize it because it is timeless. This observing faculty is apparently a natural brain function, but actually it belongs to the whole body. All that happens in our head belongs to time, because time is created by the mind. Observing in the global body belongs to the timeless.

When I speak of understanding, I mean the mind must have the right perspective, I would say the right geometrical representation, of truth. The geometrical representation shows precisely that what we are fundamentally can never be an object, can never be objectified, represented. We can never think of it. It demonstrates the limits of the mind. The mind is time, the mind is function. Time is an expression of the timeless. Time must stop to live the timeless. And when the mind has discovered its limits, then we are open to the timeless, the timeless present. We can never think of the present. We can only *be* the present. When we think of the present it is already the past, and when we try to think in the present, thought in this moment cannot find its concretization. Then there is a giving-up of representation and we live the presence in identity.

These are some ideas which we can develop and speak about. Have you anything to say?

When I first came to see you, I had the idea that I was a person with an inner life, and there was a world outside. Now it seems very clear that all this is illusion. There is no inner life, no real world outside and no person. Either there is just agitation, mental movement or no division.

But all these movements appear in your lightness, in your clearness, in your presence. All these movements have their potential in you, but you are not in them. That is why you can observe them. You are present during the activity of the mind and in the absence of the activity.

It seems so pointless that the agitation continues. There is no point to it. It's something like a wheel that was started a long time ago and has to keep spinning, but it has no meaning besides that.

You are no longer identified with it. There is nowhere to go and nobody to go, there is only open presence.

Why is there a fear of death, of letting go when there is no one who dies?

The representation of yourself as an "I," a somebody, must die. It is a reflex, nothing else. When there is fear ask, "Who has fear?" You will never find the who, you'll find only a concept called fear,

70

emotion. To see it really clearly is understanding and in this understanding you are totally free of fear. The freedom that you experience in this moment can never be localized, objectified. You can never assert it. The understanding may be in the head, but being the understanding has no longer anything to do with the head; it is your global feeling.

If it is not in the head, could one understand but not know that one understands?

You need the clear representation that you can never objectify what you are because you are it, you are the ultimate subject. You can never objectify happiness or peace or love. You can never fix them in the frame of the mind. So there is a natural giving up. You give up the head, you feel your globality.

I've read over and over again that I'm free and I'm happy right now, but how can I really know it?

There is not a knower. You can never know it, just be it.

And of course in my grasping it's not there.

The grasping is a reflex.

You say it's a reflex, but that does not mean anything to me.

You taste the flavor of the apple you eat. It is an object, but you can never have happiness; you can only be happiness. There is nothing to grasp or to take. You want to appropriate something to yourself. You want to make it your own. It is the grasping reflex which hinders you from simply being it.

That's what's so frustrating; I want it.

It is already here.

It is already here, yes, but the mind must know that, so the mind has got to keep on grasping until it gets tired of grasping and something happens . . . or has it already happened?

71

It happens when there is nothing to take, and no more appropriating to yourself, then all the energy that was used in taking comes to a stop.

Automatically?

Automatically. Then your presence refers to itself, but this presence can never be smelled or felt. You cannot take it, hear it, see it.

But could the mind still be grasping, trying to relate to the objective world, but behind the grasping you are really the happiness? Can the two co-exist? In other words, can I be happiness and just not know it?

The grasping habit may reappear from time to time, but in the end you no longer use it, because it has no more role to play. There is no more profit to be gained by it. The patterns may continue to come up, but you don't use them any more. You find yourself functioning without a functioner, without a controller.

And the body-mind functions automatically?

Yes, but don't appropriate this functioning to a functioner, to a doer.

Well, this is an illusion dispelled . . . I've always thought that I function, but I see that function goes on regardless of who I think I am.

Yes, you live in your glory and the functioning appears in your beingness, in your glory.

So all the functioning that's going on is part of my glory?

Yes, yes; there is no personal entity in the cosmos. A personal entity doesn't exist.

And what about the witness, is it apart from the mind or a function of the mind?

Witnessing is not a function. It is simply the knower. It is presence.

It's actually awareness. In other words it means the same thing: attention, witnessing, awareness.

Yes. Understand that you can only be happiness, you can never objectify it. You can never say, "I am happy," because when you say, "I am happy" you have made a state, an object, of it. The same is the case with love, or joy, or peace. You cannot objectify it, you cannot think it. You must not try to put it in the frame of the mind. Simply ignore the mind.

Sir, when you speak and when I read your words and I'm at home, there is from time to time a moment that is for me like a bubble popping. That would be one way to describe it, where my mind knows what was. There is a moment of presence. "Presence," is that what one could call it? But as soon as I identify it, it's gone; it's like I ...something happens and then it's too late...

But too late for whom? There is confusion in you.

There's nothing to do about it, is there? I mean there is this moment of being and then there is the mind saying "there it was again." It's like a juggling act.

But you can only think the past, you can never think the present. When the situation is over you can say "this was the situation," but at the time consciousness and the object are one. So you can only be aware of the past. But that you are aware of the past means that there was a witness to it. And as two functions cannot exist, it proves to you that the witnessing is not a function. Witnessing is your presence.

Are you saying that there is no such thing as individuality in consciousness?

Individuality appears in consciousness. It is also a vehicle, an expression of consciousness.

What is it then that distinguishes this location in space? Or any other location in space?

On the level of the body-mind there is multiplicity, but on the level of being there is only oneness. All living beings are one. On the level of the body-mind there are variations, but only variations in quantity. The quality is everywhere the same. It is a question of degree, not a question of quality. All beings have the same quality, virtually, and some of them actually. Some have actualized it, but virtually, potentially, the same quality is in every human being. So when you have realized your real nature, there are no others; there is only oneness.

I suppose what I find confusing is that if being is everything, then why isn't it realized everywhere?

All that is quantity and quality is in your awareness waiting for actualization, but it is there. But for you, it is important that you go much deeper into the question, "Who am I?" Live with the question. We can never find a specific answer, it is the living with it which is the answer.

Why does my self-image, self-representation, keep reappearing? Is there something in it that is trying to bring me to realize that I am not it? Is it part of the wholeness to show me who I am?

When you think of an activity, this activity refers to a non-activity and when you think of a non-activity, it refers to an activity. Any attempt to do or to not do, to achieve or to empty your mind, belongs to the mind. So you must come to the absence of non-activity, the absence of the absence. Then you are in the timeless. You will be solicited very often in daily life to be it. Give all your heart and freedom and love to it, to these timeless moments. Ignore the person, ignore the personality.

Dr. Klein, it would seem that the mind has very little hold over me. I can see it, I think, for what it is and yet the body still has a hold on me. Now I understand, or have been led to understand, that the body only comes into existence because of the mind. If that is so, does it mean that I am deluding myself in thinking that the mind no longer has any hold on me?

You can never separate the mind from the body, nor the body from the mind.

So, if I really do see the mind as being of no importance, how then do I see the body as being of no importance?

The body is a percept, you perceive it, you feel it and the mind conceptualizes it. But both come together as body-mind. You are the knower of the body-mind. I would enquire, "Who is the knower?" Don't try to find the knower in the known, or the knowing in the known. It is the body-mind which wakes up in the morning, but what you are already fundamentally is. The body-mind wakes up in your "isness," in your beingness.

It seems that I can't really do anything about this; it just has to happen of it's own accord. Is that so?

It is enough for you to know that the body-mind appears in you, lives in you, but that you are not in the body-mind. If you would be of the same substance as the body-mind, then you could never be aware of the body-mind. The body-mind, its substance, is in you, in your awareness, but you are not in the substance. You are more than the body-mind. That is why you can perceive it. It is enough that you become aware of those moments, which are timeless moments, before the body-mind wakes up in the morning. You will feel presence before the body-mind wakes. Every morning you create the body-mind, every morning you create the world.

I feel I have some vague understanding of that, and yet I still feel an attachment. Even though I can see the attachment for what it is, it still seems to be there. There is still identification, even though I have an intellectual understanding that it only exists through consciousness.

The moment you speak of certain functions of your-body mind it means that you are out of the process. When you are out of the process you use the body-mind in the right way. You know the quality of your body-mind. You know its capital. As long as you have this vehicle you use it in the right way. And identifying yourself with your vehicle causes suffering.

I don't understand what you mean when you say we create the world.

When you are in deep sleep, where is the world for you?

It appears to me that when I'm not thinking, it is not.

When you are in deep sleep, the world does not exist for you. The world appears when the body-mind appears because the body-mind belongs to the world. I would not even say that you create the world. You create your *own* world which gives security for your ego, for your "I," for the "me."

Are you saying that we imagine our world?

The world, in a certain way, is your imagination. When you wake up in your real nature, you will see an entirely other world. You create the world from moment to moment.

You mean that if we did not do this then we would be in the real world?

When we observe how we function, we see that we create the world through our choice, through our selection.

Oftentimes when I read what you have written, there is a paralysis of action and it seems to point to a stillness that almost denies action and I wonder where the source of action genuinely comes from in our lives. I go to work day by day and some of my actions are motivated by what I want to grasp, by what I desire, but there must be some fundamental source of action. Can you say something about action and how it occurs in the stillness?

You must accept it as a fact that your fundamental nature is stillness. It is in this stillness that all activities appear. Activity and non-activity belong to the mind, but stillness has nothing to do with the mind. The mind appears in stillness; the mind is an expression of stillness, is an emanation, an expansion of stillness. When you accept it as a fact, it is secondhand information, of course, but it opens you to this new dimension—that there is something beyond activity and non-activity. That is enough.

Often in daily life, there are moments of non-activity, but you qualify them as an absence of activity and do not see they are the presence of silence. This silence, you can only be it. But it is enough for you to know that there is presence, out of which arise every activity and non-activity.

So don't try to make stillness another form of experience. The moment you try to be still you create an activity. Trying to be still is an activity. Practically speaking, activity and non-activity appear to you. Don't interfere.

How can this body-mind that I'm usually identified with, how can it really touch those broader, more global moments of consciousness that appear? It seems that everything goes through this body-mind. It is I who am talking about consciousness, it's not consciousness talking about consciousness.

But the body-mind experience appears in your consciousness, appears in your stillness. The body-mind is perceived. Bring the perceived body-mind back to the perceiver. Every object is seen, every object is heard. Bring it back to the seeing, bring it back to the hearing. It is the perceived, the object, which reveals the perceiver, the ultimate subject. You can never perceive perceiving. It is here and now, reality. In this globality is perception, instantaneous, original perception.

It's as though the body-mind becomes transparent in some measure. I guess my question still is what to make of the word. I'm touched when I read the words and I'm touched when I hear the words, yet it's not the words, it's the stillness, as you say.

The words are vehicles, symbols, more or less a convention between you and me. The word is a pointer. It is really dramatic for you to hear that the perceived object can bring you back to the perceiving. But this perceiving "I" can never be perceived. You may have some idea of it, but you are not familiar with feeling your totality completely objectless, completely non-localized, in openness, in nowhere. Your openness is still open to something, but when the openness becomes completely relaxed, completely free from memory, from expectation, then this openness refers to itself.

This seeing, this hearing refers to itself. Remember that if there were not a perceiver, you could not perceive.

How is it possible to feel myself objectless? When I look at you there is direction; when I raise my hand there is intention. Very often I'm daydreaming, completely lost. The few times I feel myself in space, I feel my weight, I feel sensation, I feel tension. It is an object, it is not objectless.

Yes, it is an object perceived, but you know it, you are the perceiver. You know the feeling of space around you, you feel the weight or the absence of weight, you feel your energy, you can project your energy, you can project your body in space. All this belongs to you. You know it. The body-mind has no existence in itself. It needs consciousness. You are presence before the body-mind wakes up in the morning. The body-mind is more or less a superimposition on your awareness. That you are here, that you are looking for real equanimity, for peace and joy is because you have had a glimpse of it and this glimpse certainly comes from deep sleep, or a moment of insight which also belongs to this non-state of sleep. So the body-mind has no reality in itself, because it depends on consciousness. It is something tremendous to wake up in nothingness.

I wake up to tensions, to agitation and to thoughts, weight, movement.

All appears and disappears in nothingness, which may also be qualified as fullness.

So when the body-mind dies, stillness, consciousness is?

Stillness is, it is possible that one could perhaps remember when one was born, when the body-mind was born, but you can never remember your real birth. *It* was not born and so can never die.

So when you are awake in your real nature there is no need to prepare for death?

When you are awake in life there is no death. But I would say you can prepare your dying every evening before going to sleep. We die every evening and we wake up every morning. And not only then. We wake up from moment to moment. But what is interesting is to die knowingly. Before going to sleep give up all your qualities. Feel yourself in complete nakedness. Then before the body-mind wakes up again you will also feel yourself in this nakedness. It is exactly the same nakedness as before a thought appears and in which a thought disappears; it is the same as the space between two perceptions. The screen remains, it is there from morning to night, but the images on the screen change.

WHEN I'M SITTING IN THE GARDEN, *or on an airplane, there is a sense of . . . there is consciousness, there is stillness. And thoughts pass through, and people, and there is no problem.*

Because in stillness, in consciousness, there is nobody. For whom could it be a problem? The problem appears the moment you establish a personal relationship with the situation. When the situation is convenient for you, you identify yourself with it. And when it is not, you push it away. Convenient and not convenient belong to the mind. *Alors*, what is the question?

The question is, in stillness there is no question. In activity, as the day goes on and one speaks with people or reads or does other activities, there seems to be an identification which takes place. Sometimes suddenly there is an awareness that an identification has taken place. And then there is stillness again. My question is that it seems so strange that the identification takes place after the fact. I don't understand why that movement continues. Sometimes it seems to be habit, sometimes it seems to be something else. Because the stillness seems to be the natural state. Stillness seems to be . . .

In other words, how can we be this stillness permanently?

Yes.

It is only when you see the mechanism, how you function, that you become aware that you take yourself for somebody. The person comes in the play; the mind splits into positive and negative, pleasure and pain, and so on, and the reflex comes up to be somebody, to take yourself for what you are not. Then there is object to object relationship, relationship from personality to personality. Then, there is a problem, because this object lives for security, recognition, the need to be loved. There is only asking, demanding. At first you will see the conflict, the identification, after the situation. Then you may see it during the identification and, at the end, you will catch it before the reflex comes up.

This morning during the meditation you used the words, "organic memory." It seems to be a paradox. I thought you were calling us to feel something in the present, yet you used the words "organic memory," and memory refers to the past. I'm wondering if you would make more explicit how you are using the terminology?

When the body-mind wakes up in the morning, it is memory which wakes up. It is all your fear, anxiety, reactions, all the residues. This is the old body pattern. When you see this, you will become aware of a new body, a new sensation of the body. This is the original organic feeling. For the moment, keep this body alive. Don't go in the old pattern of feeling.

This new body is still memory? Is there a body that is not memory?

I would say that all is memory.

Except the awareness in which it arises?

Yes.

So that the new body is an organic memory, a genetic memory, as opposed to the body which is a psychological memory. Is that what you mean?

What do you think about it?

I like it. (laughter) It is an organic memory . . . It seems like living in genetic material being manifested moment to moment, but still it is manifesting in awareness. It seems then that, really, the only purpose for working with the energy body is to evoke the health of the physical organism. But, secondly, really it just refers continually back to awareness.

In working with the energy body, the muscles function in a different way.

In working on the energy body, is it possible to trigger an unbearable amount of energy that is just beyond the limits of endurance?

I have not really understood the question.

I have experienced this—presumably it is energy, because it is not localized. It permeates the whole body, and the feeling is so intense that it is unbearable. It could be bearable, if one didn't get frightened. I thought possibly that this might happen in a meditative situation.

All nervous manifestation of energy is an elimination of residues of tension. Come back to the original state of sensation. Come back, don't follow it.

It doesn't manifest itself in strong feeling then?

The more that you live in the vital body, the more elastic it is, the more dynamic.

I keep asking the same question. I find that as I get more open, allowing myself to be more open in awareness, that sometimes there is a kind of fear that comes up that doesn't seem to be triggered by any thought, but seems to be a kind of old memory in the body of an old time in this lifetime or another lifetime, who knows. I'm saying this lifetime probably, when there was a fear of letting-go, a very deep fear, a survival fear of letting-go, a fear that if the organism let go that somehow it would die. That memory seems to be deep in the body. So when I experience letting-go, at a certain point it is almost as if the body freezes. Then it becomes very difficult to be open, to remain open, to open to fear, to open to sensations, to open to

83

anything. It is almost as if the whole organism shuts down. I wonder how or what to do in that moment. I have heard you say to be aware of the sensations and set aside conceptualization. Yet at these moments there are no concepts particularly. It usually feels like—I don't even know where to begin to be open. It is almost as if that doesn't make any sense in that moment. Sometimes it lasts for quite a while.

In this passage of letting-go there is still a sensation of pain. The residues of which you are speaking are very deep rooted. When the residues are completely eliminated, you will feel an absence. This absence may feel near to pain for a very short moment. But then there is immediate release. It is only through awareness that you become aware of it; it is only through awareness that elimination is possible.

By residues do you mean residues in the body?

Yes, when there is no conceptualization.

In those moments it doesn't feel like anything is being eliminated, in fact it feels as if things are holding on in a very strong way. I don't feel an elimination. First I feel an elimination, a relaxation, a letting-go, a kind of clarity. Then there is the sense of . . . no bottom, nothing to hold onto. In that there is a fear, a fear that there is nothing to hold onto. That stimulates it—some old body memory. So that even when I set aside the ideas something is still . . .

The body can never change by itself. It is consciousness which produces the change. In this moment it is a pure perception, a direct perception.

So just be with that perception?

Yes.

What happens in those moments when I try to be with the direct perception is that I seem to get lost in it and it intensifies. It gets more and more intense. Rather than feeling relaxed and spacious and open, there is a sense—it is almost as if the mind goes into it and intensifies it, becomes almost an accomplice to it and intensifies it. So then I start to get lost. I don't know what to do with the mind. Then I start to try to figure out what to do with the mind and then it becomes an act of will. So . . .

In this pure perception there is no conceiving, there is only perceiving. You are completely free when there is a fusion of the perceiver and the perceived. When a fusion has taken place between the perceiver and the perceived, then the operation has taken place; it is finished. So you must be completely one.

With the sensation?

Yes. Do not interfere with your convoluted mind.

In the past, I have heard you say that rather than interfere with the mind, to create a space for the sensation in which it unfolds.

Absolutely. Let it dissolve.

And wherever it goes, if it intensifies let it do what it does?

Absolutely. It is a timeless moment, because it is free from the mind conceiving it, qualifying it.

So one does not pay attention . . . when the fusion takes place, it just takes place. It is not created by effort or practice. It is like something given.

Yes. It takes place.

The whole room has changed completely.

Absolutely. There is only waiting without anticipation. When you look back, you will see that the chessboard has completely changed. The queen is somewhere else.

Is there an element of biological survival in the body's reaction to letting-go? Just now, Stephan was saying that as he goes to deeper and deeper layers of relaxation or expansion, there come moments of getting stuck or blocked or paralyzed. It is like a veil that must be lifted before you go to the next expansion. Is there any element of biological survival that comes up at that moment—the survival of the body? For example, I think the reason we can go to sleep so easily, go to our beds and go to sleep, is because we take it for granted that we will wake up in the morning. If we didn't think we would wake up in the morning, we would probably not go to sleep in the same way. So I'm wondering if biological survival comes in at these moments where there is a kind of paralysis in letting-go, or is it only psychological?

It is only psychological.

There is another important aspect to your question that I would like to ask. You referred to moving through to deeper layers of expansion. I really want to hear something about that because, to me, it has the connotation of the progressive way. Do we in fact move through layers of expansion?

When you familiarize yourself with attention without expectation, letting the attention simply be attentive, there is unfolding, unfolding in alertness, in intelligence, until it comes to what we call awareness. There is no growing in awareness, because in growing there is dynamism which belongs to the mind, to the progressive way. Be attuned to the awareness, one with it; don't emphasize what you are aware of. There is no one aware and nothing of which you are aware.

IN ACCEPTING A SITUATION we are completely free. Accepting unfolds in beingness. In accepting a situation we accept the situation in our completeness. Accepting is not in the mind; I would say it is beyond the mind, because the mind can never accept. In accepting it is not the situation we emphasize, we emphasize the accepting itself. This brings us complete freedom, openness. It is only in accepting a situation that we see what the situation is, what the facts are. Then action comes out of the situation, out of the facts. The decision to act doesn't go through the mind. It is spontaneous. In the accepting position, there is no volition, because in accepting there is no place for an ego, for an "I."

Have you anything to say?

When we are caught up in a situation, how do we make the shift from being caught up to being in attention? It seems that we need volition to make an effort to get out of the situation in which we are caught up, and if I make an effort I'm caught up in effort and volition.

But you must not try to get out of the situation, because your trying will just replace the situation. You are then as bound as before. Accepting the situation is the nearest that you can do. That is the beginning!

But at that moment, I don't know what accepting looks like.

It's not psychological accepting, it is functional accepting. It is accepting in the way a scientist accepts the facts of the problem to be resolved. When you accept the facts in this way, you will find yourself out of the situation. You will be in the accepting feeling, not in what you accept, the object, the situation. Accepting means accepting every fact, every perception that comes to you. It means accepting your reactions as part of the facts. Then see how the accepting acts on you: How do you feel in this accepting? Is there a freedom you experience?

An openness.

Yes, openness.

And that's what you're looking for, this openness? So do you find that you were not looking for a solution as such, the solution is almost a side effect of the welcoming? You discover that it was the accepting, the welcoming, you were looking for?

Absolutely.

But there is something right there that I don't understand, because it is a fact that my mind is always looking for solutions; so if I truly accept the facts, it means I must also accept that the mind is looking for solutions. Or does the mind somehow change and stop looking for solutions?

Accepting is not in the mind.

I understand that, but what I am saying is that it sounds as though if I accept, then everything is going to be fine. But the mind may still be agreeing or disagreeing and the feelings may still be reacting, and in some way I may still have to be this person that I call "me." I can't walk out of it, and I can't exactly walk into it any more, so it still has to come out of me. I have to do something, or not do something. Some choice has to be made.

This harmonization of the mind is done by the accepting. It is the accepting of the situation which harmonizes the situation. The mind, feelings and so on share in the totality, in the integrality.

When the emphasis is on the accepting itself, the mind and body function appropriately.

What is important is for you to see how accepting acts on you. Make the accepting position an object of your observation. Take note of how you feel and function when you are in welcoming.

One of the reasons I asked that question is because I have met people who are apparently very accepting, but they are not really accepting; it's just a kind of passivity. It's as though they say: I won't look at the situation to see what is really going on. They seem to have no energy left.

Accepting is free from volition, and absolutely active, alert. It is passive-active.

How can one go from being caught in the situation to accepting it? You are aware that you do not accept the facts. You know yourself, your choice and selection, you know how choice is conflict. You are aware how a situation belongs to your security; how you accept it when it belongs to your security and you refuse it and escape it when you judge that it does not bring you security. You know perfectly that there are many egos hiding in you.

But accepting is when you say, "I don't know."

It must be a magic moment.

Very magic. It is a real explosion when you say, "I accept the situation, I accept the fact." Then you are completely free of personal interference.

When I look at a situation, where I am struggling, then all of a sudden there is a moment where I realize I am struggling and I don't know what to do, and I'm caught, and I look around for something to do. And then in some way there is a memory of how it occurred in the past. And that somehow gives me a little perspective, and then it feels like a relaxation, and then this explosion. Would you have any other way of describing this?

You must accept all your different reactions and then the situation unfolds in your accepting.

89

In learning acceptance, I have come up against the problem of taking an initiative, of initiating action. Because, if I understand acceptance rightly, you accept whatever life brings to you. Now does that mean you don't actually initiate actions; or do you accept the fact that you need to initiate an action? If I may give you an example that may help to explain it: I came to America to hear you. I could have stayed in England to hear you later on this year. So I initiated an action which in one sense seems to me to be wrong because I didn't accept the fact that I was actually in England. This is very tortuous, it is an example of something I need to understand better. Does one go through life just accepting what comes to one, or can one at times go out and initiate things that are not strictly necessary to one's living?

The solution comes in the accepting.

Does that mean that all I have to do is to accept that I wanted to come to America?

Yes.

Thank you. May I clarify that? I didn't want to come to America; I wanted to come to see Dr. Klein.

Is one way to look at it that each of us is really the ultimate, the pure consciousness, but it is not known to us? It may come at any time to any one of us, at any moment. Whether we accept, whether we are in sensation, whether we believe or not. It may come to us. But the likelihood may be low, and things like accepting, moving with sensation, doing pranayama, these things may make it more available in a certain sense?

In accepting one is empty. But in your accepting there is still some expectation. Real accepting is a letting-go, a giving-up, a waiting. Waiting without waiting.

What is the purpose of objects, of creation?

All that we call objects are expressions, extensions of life. But objects are not life, they are the expressions of life. Objects are only to point us to the ultimate subject. Their only meaning is to reveal the ultimate subject, to glorify the ultimate subject, as in music, painting, architecture, poetry. There's no purpose in it.

Is that what you mean when you say it's like a film? To you, in timeless awareness, all the things that are going on are like us going to movies?

You see the film, but you don't belong to the film. What you call your existence belongs to the film. But your consciousness doesn't belong to the film. So don't identify yourself with your film. Be what you are.

Accepting reaches even your heart. There's a surrender. It is beyond time when you accept the situation. It reaches all your being, it acts tremendously on you. You would like to see a meaning and a purpose in all this, but it is only a play. But perhaps you are too serious to understand that. (laughter)

You have referred to a state beyond objects, an experience of emptiness which you call a blankness that occurs as a result of progressive practice. You spoke of it as tragic, or even as the dark night of the soul, but then later you spoke of fullness. I was wondering if you could speak of that transition, if it is possible, between this emptiness and fullness.

When I speak of emptiness I mean empty of the past; it is only fullness when there's a complete absence of the past. But when you focus on eliminating objects you will be stuck to the absence of objects rather than the fullness behind absence and presence.

I still don't understand how there can be action in total acceptance.

The impulse to act is sudden, the execution takes place in time and space, taking into consideration all that you have at your disposal, mental, physical, material, etc. To execute the impulse to act calls for intelligence.

But I always experience confusion when carrying out the impulse. I see all these images of Christ on the cross. Is there a way in which we cherish suffering and that image is like an image of the whole self? I see that what

I'm frightened of losing somehow is the separateness which is causing me the problem.

I have not followed the question.

I was just saying that when I see the images of Christ, he seems to me to embody the suffering of separateness. And I wondered if there is a way in which I cherish suffering because I cherish separateness?

But what we are fundamentally is oneness. There is no separateness between you and me. The only separateness is that you take yourself for somebody. If you would take yourself for nothing you would be one with me. There is no "me," there is no other.

Sometimes you say it is a complete absence, and that really strikes me—to be completely absent of myself.

Do not glorify the absence, it is simply absence. In the absence of yourself there is presence. You can only find yourself in your absence.

Can objects disappear in your presence, in a sense individually, or is it that the whole objective field is absorbed at once?

An object has its homeground in your awareness. It is in the nature of the object to go back to its homeground, to the perceiving. An object only exists in you. It is you who project the object.

Going back to the subject of acceptance, I have played with that a little bit in my life. I've experimented with it; and what I've observed is that when I take note of, for example, my co-worker's dramatic judgment and criticism of others, I see my reaction—that it's upsetting to me. But when I can move to a place of being more objective, I realize that I don't have to change her—in any case I can't. But I also then accept my discomfort with that and then take a deep breath and let it go, and it's as if I watch parts of my ego kind of diminish. But it's not easy to do.

Yes, but your ego is a contraction; the ego frees itself in deep relaxation, but ordinarily it stays there.

Well it certainly feels different when I . . .

When you are relaxed.

Relaxed, yes.

Because in this relaxation there is letting-go. In accepting a situation there's a letting-go. Letting-go means letting go of your volition, your interference. There's also love in this accepting.

You say that fundamentally we are all one; and I guess we realize that we are happy, we're free from suffering, but even if we don't realize it and we suffer, what does it matter anyway since we are all one?

But you can note that the ultimate subject has identified itself with a suffering object. Taking yourself for what you are not creates suffering.

And trying to get out of it creates suffering too?

Of course. Your suffering is fundamentally because you feel yourself isolated. The moment you objectify yourself you are contracted. But be careful about taking yourself for nothing! Taking yourself for nothing is also something. So there must be a double absence of nothingness. (laughter)

What I observe in myself is that when I'm in a place of isolation and suffering, I see that my mind then starts to try to bridge that, and I get preoccupied with what to do with my life, so to speak; and it seems that really what one does doesn't matter all that much, that it's more how one is relating moment to moment than doing anything particular in the world. Or is there something in one's individuality that reaches some kind of fullness of expression in the world in a unique way?

What is the motive in you to express yourself? There is something in you which has an inner need to offer. A kind of thankfulness, the joy to be. In your case, writing is an offering for allowing to be.

I seem to run into a part of myself that won't allow that offering, that thinks there ought to be something else that is more important to me.

93

The offering is already accomplished in even a quick look in the eyes. You don't *need* to do anything.

I notice in the body-work that the body finds a limit of comfort, but then it can go a bit further and a bit further if I am very relaxed. So, I wondered whether it is a biological or psychological limit. Could it be possible, if one were to remove the psychological limits, to go back to some point of being supple, such as one had experienced in adolescence or even babyhood? Is it possible for this old body, if the psychological limits were removed, to go back to being younger?

There is also some biological stop, not only psychological. But it's important that you feel the posture.

Is it acceptance, not a case of trying to achieve extended limits?

Yes, yes.

And that's in a sense what the body-work is about?

Yes. But don't worry about the body-work. Take note of the many moments when you are without any question.

I don't understand.

There are many moments when you have no questions.

No questions?

Yes, so you are a happy man in a certain way.

There aren't many moments like that. (laughter) There's always a question: Where am I going, what am I doing, what's it all about?

Yes.
(pause)

Is it useful when walking along to try to sense the energy body ahead of one, projecting the body first as one moves?

Absolutely.

94

In all directions?

Yes.

That would help to develop an understanding again.

Yes, in a certain way when you are in your car, you are more than five meters in front of your car already. When jogging you are several meters in front with your energy body.

I've always thought it was the mind that was in front.

It's also the energy body.

Does the mind take the energy body along?

The mind is only looking for a result. When you are jogging there is no mind, there is only energy in your body, the breathing, the elasticity, all the reactions. Jogging properly is a very high art. When jogging you should never put your foot on the floor. Never. Running belongs to the games of the Greeks. According to the paintings, in those days runners were portrayed only in the lateral position; there was no verticality. In a certain way they were flying. It's a very high art to run well.

When the San Francisco 49ers won the Super Bowl, I was in a bar with 300 people who were screaming in great ecstasy and joy as the final time ended and San Francisco won. I was thinking at that time that everybody was out of their minds, and in the self. Do you think that's true? (laughter)

The Super Bowl is . . . I don't know what the French equivalent is. (laughter) Maybe this is a frivolous question.
(silence)

Is the relationship you mentioned yesterday, a relationship between the physical body and the vital body, energy body, still there when there is sickness? Is the energy body always whole, or does sickness manifest itself somehow in that energy body too?

In Chinese medicine the energy body is divided into several other bodies. When we speak here of the energy body, it is more or less the elastic body. The elasticity of the body is joyful.

The physical body cannot be separated from the energy body. There is only energy. The energy of the physical body is more condensed, but the vital and physical bodies interpenetrate each other. When the energy body is completely felt, completely alive, the physical body becomes free from reactions and is harmonious. The energy flows then without hindrance.

W̲HAT IS LOOKING FOR YOU IS YOU. It is looking for itself. When you say, "I have understood" you haven't understood, because you are still living with the material of non-understanding. You may have a real geometrical representation of the understanding, but this material is located in the mind. This geometrical representation must dissolve in being the understanding. And being the understanding is when you are completely free from the mind; when you live your freedom, free from the "I," the "me," the non-understanding.

When understanding concerns a new object, you refer the non-understanding to certain objects that you already know. But when it comes to understanding what you are, the ultimate subject, which can never be referred to any object, this understanding must dissolve completely in being the understanding. So it is important that we wait for being the understanding; wait without any representation. Because what you are fundamentally can never be represented, can never be imagined.

The geometrical representation is the clear seeing, the total conviction that you are the ultimate subject and that this subject can never be objectified. This clear seeing automatically orients you because you see that all you are hoping for, looking for, striving for—all that is attainable—is an object. This geometrical understanding brings you to an absolute giving-up of all looking for

97

states, experiences, teachers, achievements. You see very clearly that what you are looking for is your nearest, that you can only live with your very nearest and all accumulation of knowledge and information is a going away from what you are fundamentally.

Have you something to say about it?

Does this geometrical understanding take place in ordinary thinking or is it a totally other kind of process?

Geometrical understanding does not take place in ordinary thinking, which deals only with objects. The ordinary mind functions only in representation. Ordinary thinking is only in terms of the senses. When thinking starts from thinking, from a thought, you remain in thought, in the linear framework. This happens in functional thinking, calculative thinking, rational thinking. But in what we call creative thinking, thinking that points to the ultimate subject—this thinking starts from non-thinking. It is a looking away from thinking. It starts from silence.

Creative thinking does not start from an object, but it still deals with objects. Higher reason concerns only the ultimate subject. Geometrical understanding is that you see beyond a shadow of doubt that you are not an object. I call it "geometrical" because there is an almost mathematical representation of what objects are, and that the subject of these objects is not an object. At first you see an object and take yourself for the relative subject in relation to the object. As long as you take yourself for the relative subject there is still a witness. But when you see that the relative subject is an object too, then all emphasis is taken off objects and they dissolve in your observing, the ultimate subject. Then the witness disappears, because the witness and the ultimate subject are one.

So understanding dissolves completely in your totality. You can never represent it. Atmananda Krishna Menon said, "You will feel it without feeling it." And my teacher said, "You will know it without knowing it."

It makes sense to me that striving for an object is pointless. But I've been feeling as though I have to use effort to be alert. I'm sure that's not right, but I feel I have to wake myself up.

You should take it from me, as secondhand information, that what you are looking for—you already are. When you take that stance as your starting point, you will become aware of all the effort expended in end-gaining, achieving, becoming. Accepting this secondhand information brings you to look at the energy that accompanies the becoming process. When you see it, you are no longer an accomplice to this becoming, this waste of energy. You let go, at a certain moment, of all anticipation, all end-gaining. It is not a voluntary giving-up; it gives up itself. And in this moment you are free from all activities. This moment refers to itself. In other words, poetically speaking, you are taken. But you must first take it for your own that what you are looking for—you already are.

Is the energy body something we are imagining?

Let's not be stuck to the word energy body. This morning we proceeded through movements, we were aware of the movement. Being aware here means we go from one point to another point. What we generally do is that from one point we already anticipate the next point. We are not present to the movement. We overlook and push through many hindrances and then say the movement is accomplished. This anticipation, impatience, is violence. We can say this process is completely mechanical.

In these sessions we discover that our structure has the capacity to be felt. We feel the sensation. When we feel the sensation, the muscle, the structure, appears to us completely differently. It loses its heaviness. It loses its density. And we become aware of another level in our body which is dynamic, elastic. When we use this elastic body, this tactile sensation, we can never anticipate. We are obliged to go from moment to moment, or rather, to *be* from moment to moment. In moving in this way, there is no hindrance.

This feeling sensation gives life to the cell. It opens the cell. This feeling energy, this feeling sensation, we can maintain with our sensitivity; but first we must discover it in our body. It is the vital difference between a mechanical movement and a felt, a conscious, movement.

You have spoken of several levels or sheaths of the body . . .

Sensitivity takes us beyond the physical body. When you become aware of these other layers of energy, you are open to intelligence. Intelligence refers to the deeper levels. But you have the impression that all these layers are in your expansion.

You feel it also in the experience of meditation. Generally when we think of meditation we think of it as a kind of introversion, in-going; a kind of withdrawing the senses, to interiorize all the senses. I would say you often concentrate, go to a center, get stuck, end up blocked. There may be a kind of stillness, certainly. Perhaps, for a certain moment, there's an absence of thinking, an absence of acting; but this absence keeps you bound, keeps you in fixation.

In any form of introverted meditation, the "I," the "me," is still there. And because the meditator is still there, it creates an object, a state, an experience. But when you have understood that the "I," the "me," the person, is nothing but a contraction, a fixation, with the giving-up of the person you will find yourself in expansion. Exactly the opposite happens—instead of concentrating, withdrawing, you let go, you expand, you dissolve completely in this expansion. And in this dissolving, in this expansion, the sheaths, the different energy layers become actualized. They are freed from fixation, and blossom. So in meditation we are nothing other than openness, a total, global "I don't know," in being the knowing.

You have spoken of the importance of being in the heart, of the heart as the final door. How does this relate to what Ramana Maharshi called the heart on the right side?

He may experience the center where time meets the timeless in this way. It is the same as the symbolism of the cross where you will see

100

the timeless in the vertical, and where horizontal time meets the timeless. Where time meets the timeless—that is the heart.

The timeless is in the now. The point when the horizontal meets the vertical is in the now. It is in the heart center. The head belongs to time. You can never experience the timeless in the head. The heart is the timeless. It is only at this point that there is presence. It is being knowledge.

You can have this experience immediately. It immediately dissolves the experiencer. And then it is a non-experience that is not in subject-object relationship.

It is only in the heart, it is only in this expansion, in your homeground, that there is meditation, that there is openness from moment to moment. There is seeing, the eyes are open; there is hearing, the ears are open; there is smelling, the nostrils are open. All the organs function according to necessity, but meditation is from moment to moment.

In the heart there is no place for a person. All that appears in your surroundings refers to your wholeness, your completeness. There are no more psychological reactions. There is no more choice, no more selection, because you no longer stand in the mind. Your stand is in consciousness. When you take your stand knowingly in consciousness there are no more problems. There may be functional difficulties, but there is nothing problematic. But the moment you look from the point of view of the mind there are problems, there is choice. And when there is choice there is suffering.

What happens to consciousness after the death of the body?

Consciousness is. Consciousness is life. All that exists, all that is perceived, are expressions, prolongations of life, of consciousness. But consciousness is.

Can consciousness ever die?

Never. What is not born can never die. So there is no real meaning to think about death. All we can do is to discover, to explore life.

101

The expressions appear in this continuity, in time. But consciousness, what you are fundamentally, is free from time. The timeless knows nothing about past and future. What we call time is in succession. But when you are in the timeless this succession doesn't exist. It is absolutely in the now.

So concerning death, until you really discover life the problem of death is completely meaningless. It is only an idea. And when you know life, when you are in the timeless, it does not even come to you to think of death.

Does living knowingly make any difference when we die? Is there anything left of individuality at death? Is there reincarnation of the energy body?

The energy body goes to energy. The etheric body goes to the etheric. The astral goes to the astral, and so on. They dissolve. But consciousness is. There is nobody to go somewhere. Because there is nowhere to go, and nobody to go.

How we die is important. But wondering what happens after death is a movement from the "I," from the supposed "me." It is still living with an idea. Karma! For whom? As long as you believe you are somebody, there is karma.

There seem to be so many choices. Choices are a dilemma. What to eat? Where to sit? To come to the seminar? To buy what kind of computer? Whom to marry?

Whether to have a cat? (laughter)

You mentioned a geometrical understanding and a living understanding. What is the connection between the two?

It is the geometrical representation which dissolves the non-understanding. Geometrical understanding is still a mind activity, built up with the same stuff as non-understanding, but perfectly free from memory. Each seeing, which is a combination of logic and insight, is a new experience. So this geometrical understanding must dissolve in being the understanding.

The ultimate question comes up when there is a certain maturity. This question often takes the form, "Who am I?" This question will stay until it is completely dissolved in the understanding which is the answer. Because the question *is* the answer. And it is the answer forever. There is no longer any return.

But in living with the question you will have the fore-feeling that the mind can never understand the question.

Once the mind has started to lose its hold, will everything else just happen?

You can have it now.

Is clarity of the mind with geometrical understanding a necessary pre-requisite?

When there is geometrical clarity of the mind, the mind is bathed in the answer. It has the quality of being the understanding and there can be no more return to ignorance. There may still be residues of the "I," the "me," but these residues dissolve, eliminate in time. That is certain. The understanding of truth is instantaneous, but elimination takes time.

The body-mind continues to function more or less as before, but now there is something else. When you go to Shanghai and walk through the streets you see the layout of the streets, but if you go in a plane and fly above Shanghai you will see the same streets in a completely new way.

It is new, but is it more real?

Yes, more real, more global.

The teaching is to bring us to geometrical clarity; it can't bring us to being the understanding because we are it already?

Yes. You see your life in a different way. Nobody changes, because there is nobody.

Certain behavior may completely change, but you don't change it. You are no longer stimulated by certain activities. You don't look for stimulation any more.

Life goes on in a new and unexpected way.

Why have you chosen the word geometrical? There is great feeling, symmetry, etc., to that word.

In my life I love music very much. Music appears in this geometrical form. When you go, for example, to Milano, and you want to see the dome of the cathedral, you have to take several steps backward to see and even then it is very difficult; because although the cathedral was built in a big square, all the new houses have been built too near, so it is not possible to see the Duomo as a whole. You can only go from fraction to fraction. When you go from fraction to fraction, one fraction dissolves in another fraction; one point fuses in another point. When all the points have fused together, you have a kind of geometrical representation of the whole. It no longer belongs to the eyes, it belongs to your own construction. Geometrical representation is the clear seeing of the whole. But because we only know the harmony of the whole, because we ourselves are composed in harmony; the geometrical representation dissolves in global feeling, our own harmony, and then there is the aesthetic experience. You feel it as a work of art. It is built up of elements you can see, touch and hear; but there is no longer any hold to its substance; it dissolves in beauty. This is art when there is no more hold to its materiality.

Teaching is a great art.

In a certain way, yes. But the real teaching is a non-teaching, because in reality there is nothing to teach. What you are looking for, you are fundamentally. What is there to teach?

You often talk of your teacher. How did your teacher assist you?

In teaching you use symbols, you use language. You use words built out of clarity. But there is something behind the words. When

104

you are stuck to the words you remain in the mind. That is why listening is important. It is only in listening that you find what is behind the words. In listening there is no listener; there is no reference to the mind. There is only listening, openness; open to that out of which the words arise.

Words are not the truth. What is important is what is behind the words. Words are only an echo.

Sri Atmananda said, "The guru's smile is the highest teaching."

Yes, it comes from the heart.

What good does it do us to talk or write about these things?

When you are receptive and listening, free from any reference, then you are open to the words. The spoken words are not only words, they come directly from the meaning; they bring one to the right geometrical representation. That is why it says in the sacred books that you must live with the words, the formulation of the guru, the teacher. These are in a certain way pointers to the truth.

But does it help us to create our own words of our experience, or does it take us away from the truth?

When you hear higher reasoning—higher reasoning means here, in the traditional sense, reasoning which doesn't refer to an object, which refers to the subject—when you live with it, you can find your own words which may stimulate you more, or with which you are more at home.

But live with these words as you live with the picture of your beloved. You don't need to look at it all the time. You look at it from time to time.

Are you saying that if I write a poem that comes from stillness, it is like the ultimate stillness coming back to me, and I might be able to hear that better?

Truth speaks from itself to itself.

WHAT IS OUR REAL NATURE?

Our real nature is openness, silence. It is revealed in the instantaneous understanding that truth can never be acquired. All that we look for and find is an object. It suddenly becomes clear that the seeker is the sought, that the looker is what he is looking for; then all projection to find something stops. This stopping moment cannot refer to anything other than itself. One can call it an insight, a clear understanding, or as we said yesterday, a geometrical representation of the truth. It brings a completely new orientation.

Yesterday I asked a question about choice. It suddenly came to me that there is no choice, because everywhere I look, everything I see, refers back to the silence. All objects are a reflection of that silence. They are essentially the same.

Yes, different names are given, different forms are given, but they are all the same. There are not two, there is only one.

If it is only the mind which labels objects, where is the border between one object and another?

The subject-object relationship is made by the mind. But when there is a real understanding that the seeker is the sought, it is something tremendous. When the mind understands this, it sees

107

clearly that everything it can find is an object, but our real nature is not an object and cannot be *found*. It *is*.

Is the subject-object relationship always necessary as long as there is appearance?

The subject-object relationship only exists as memory. In the moment itself we can never speak of subject and object. It is memory which says, "I saw an object." Thinking it was "me" who saw an object comes later. When you see an object, the object is a projection of the seeing.

Does that mean you can only see an object in the past?

Yes, all that the mind can understand is in the past, because consciousness is present, global seeing.

In other words, beingness is outside of what we call the historical process?

Yes.

So, love can never be found in the historical process?

No, never. Love is only in the now.

I don't understand. When we are in touch with the sensation, the energy, which is an object, I don't see that it is in the past. I see it very much in the present. It's not the mind creating it; it is an immediate experience. Something new and different is happening, and it's real.

Yes, it happens in you.

In me? But that's not the past is it, when it happens?

When it happens you are one with it. But when you name it, when you say, "I have it," there is no longer energy; there is only a concept. We cannot see an object and at the same moment say, "I see it." We cannot have two objects, two thoughts at a given time. It might appear as though we can, but when you examine the mechanism clearly, there is a rapid succession. We can only have one thought, one perception at a time. That is what I mean by "consciousness is always one with its object."

If the states of dreaming and sleep are contained within our real nature, does that mean whatever is going on in those states does not affect the present beingness, the awareness?

Dreaming, sleeping, and waking are in space and time, but you are timeless. Let us stay with our conversation which is about truth and our real nature. Let us not commit psychological evasion.

When you really see that what you are looking for is yourself, and when you find, after many years of looking down every path, trying all systems, all techniques, that you are what you are looking for, it is a tremendous revelation. Because when you really see it, you see that all these ways and experiences and techniques are only objects. You can find them but you can never find the subject, because the subject can never be objectified. In seeing this there is a stopping of looking around and all refers to this stopping moment, all refers to itself. You clearly understand that there is nowhere to go. This is a revolution in your life. It may be the Tao of thinking; "the Tao which you can find and name is not the Tao."

In your book Who Am I? *you talk about becoming aware of those instances during the day when we're in a non-state, and that as one becomes more aware of these moments they will increase. But it seems that in becoming aware of these moments, you are already out of them; so how would that make them increase?*

In the daytime there are moments when there is no activity. If, in those moments of non-activity, you don't superimpose an absence of activity, which is what we generally do, then you are completely open to a new direction. You become attuned to the moment of non-activity. When you become attuned to the moment, there is eternity. You will be solicited, you will be invited.

You will come to the understanding that your activity appears in this timelessness and there will be no more compensation. Generally, thinking is compensation, psychological evasion, living

109

in psychological time, past and future. But all this goes away and we really see what we need to see; we act according to the facts we see. But there are many moments when there is nothing to think, nothing to do.

You do not need to look for these moments of silence. They look for you. You will find yourself in moments of astonishment when you are completely open. There is no person who is astonished; there is only astonishment. Your whole being is this astonishment, because there is no reference to the past, no reference to the already known.

So when you really understand that there is nothing to find, that everything you can find is an object and a limitation; when you know that you are what you are looking for, then you will take yourself for a jewel. All your activity changes.

It seems then that there is a very dramatic shift in one's perspective. In the Gita when Krishna shows Arjuna a glimpse of himself, Arjuna sees something which is quite dramatic. Is this the same thing?

Yes.

So it seems there is a shift in emphasis from the world of objects, which we pursue and which causes a lot of suffering, to the point where the objects appear within you, and dissolve in you. Does this occur?

It is very clear that whatever you look for, whatever you can find, is only an object in space and time, nothing else. All that you can find has no existence in itself, no reality in itself, because it has no independence. It needs consciousness; it needs presence to be known. When you see this clearly, then there is a giving up. Don't go away from this moment.

It is like knowing that you have very bad eyesight and looking for your glasses everywhere, and suddenly becoming aware that they are on your nose.

Is it one moment or every moment?

Every moment; but first it is one moment, one timeless moment.

110

I would like to ask again about space and time. From my own experience I see that most of the time I'm not even aware of space and time. I'm not even in touch with what's in front of me. I can be walking down a beautiful path and not see the trees because I'm lost in a thought, an image, a memory, a fear or a tension in my body that keeps me from realizing that there is space. I may wake up half an hour later and intuitively and suddenly say, "I'm here. On this path where I am walking, there is a tree in front of me." Most of the time I'm in total fantasy, in images which have nothing to do with what's around me. I'm not even aware that I'm in space. I'm not even aware that I'm sitting on this floor, that this energy is here. Is it possible to make this leap out of fantasy? Or is there a first step which is to be not identified in some way, making me really see where I am?

But the moment you see it, you are out of space and time. In order to see that the train goes by at one hundred and twenty miles an hour, you must be out of the train.

I guess what I'm saying is that from my own observation I see that I'm generally lost in a dream.

That is enough, because then the recording has stopped.

Is that when you are being solicited by reality?

There may be moments when your constructions, your daydreams and fantasies spontaneously stop. They come to a moment's exhaustion. At this point you have to consciously continue them. But do not continue consciously. Stay with the stop. It is at this stop, this moment of exhaustion, when you are solicited.

Then do we need to allow it, welcome it? That seems to be the difficult part; we block it out or we don't even recognize it's knocking at the door.

It's no longer a question of recognizing, in the stop we are it. We may again drift away through our daydreaming, identifying ourselves with phenomenal objects; but then we again come to a stop, and it is like coming out of deep sleep. You feel a freshness, happiness, freedom.

It is important to live with a certain *representation* of truth which is what we call geometrical understanding. This is all there is to understand concerning our real nature.

What happens to the mind at the moment of that initial bliss? Does it cease to exist?

The body feels completely released.

Why do the patterns start again?

There are residues of the pattern, but you become aware of these residues. When you identify the pattern, you don't fuel it any more.

You have had this experience often in your life. You gave yourself to a certain number of activities; you gave them certain qualities, goals, hopes, and then one day you saw that all they promised was not there. So, naturally you give them up. You no longer fuel them. You simply ignore them. You did not try to change your activities, they just changed. It requires no effort.

But if you're stuck in identifying with all the residues, don't you need to make an effort to remind yourself not to identify with them, to pull yourself back?

When you have the understanding, something happens in your body. The body has an organic memory of its perfect state of relaxation and freedom. It can perfectly remember. The mind does not choose, it is the body which makes the choice. In certain moments the body feels this freedom, this ability to be completely open and absolutely intelligent. It is infinitely more pleasurable than any pleasure the mind can invent. When you do these exercises with your body, very soon the organic memory awakes and you will find the right approach. The old patterns may come up, but they have no more role to play and lose their hold.

So, you can trust that memory? You don't have to do anything?

No, you need do nothing except be sensitive to what the body tells you. To play a musical instrument well takes a certain attitude from your body. You find this attitude from organic memory.

You were talking about being solicited by truth when the mind reaches exhaustion. It seems that it's quite different from surrender. I feel when I get to that point of exhaustion that the mind goes one of two ways. Either it stays blocked psychologically, or it can let go into expansion. Can you say any more about what the key is, or what invites this solicitation?

The mind becomes exhausted because it is aware that you have enclosed yourself in a universe of concepts and beliefs. You do not feel comfortable in this conceptual universe and you try by all means to get out. Suddenly you see that this escaping from the universe of concepts and beliefs belongs to that universe and that *all* your doing keeps you a prisoner in that conceptual universe. It is a vicious circle. When you see it, there is a stop and you automatically find yourself out of the circle, but the mind can never get out of the circle by its own will. The mind can never change, evolve or work its way out of its conceptual world. All you can do is see that you are tied to it, that you feel yourself not really comfortable, that you are looking for a new direction. You are looking for a new film, a new wife, new wealth, a new job, a new philosophy of life, a new therapist. But you still remain in the same cage. All these directions are compensations to avoid the real issue: facing the stopping of doing. The moment you see this situation clearly, there is understanding. The understanding is that you are it, that you cannot find it. Then all your activity changes. You become really functional. You live in the now. You are free from psychological time, past-future. The past dies. You die to the past. You are free.

It seems to me that the key is in what we mean by seeing and what we mean by understanding. Usually my seeing does bring some changes, but it doesn't bring the radical transformation that you are talking about. The understanding I have is just partial. It comes and goes. But there are moments when I see the edge of something new. Right on the edge there is a whole new universe of understanding. But I never see it clearly. We all use the word seeing. The word seeing generally implies subject-object. It is misleading us. We all have different ways of being and of seeing. So, when you use the words seeing and understanding, if it is not mental, not emotional, not physical, what is it?

When I speak of seeing, it means being it—being completely attuned with it. You will see that you do not act in your daily life according to your understanding. You still use the old patterns. You are not in tune with your understanding.

The question is how to come out of the old pattern, to behave according to this understanding with your surroundings. When you behave according to this understanding, you are not psychologically involved. You see the situation from a completely new point of view. When you see the world from the point of view of the body, the world is nothing other than your five senses. When you see it from your sixth sense, the mind, you conceptualize the world. With both of these there is conflict. But when you see the world from consciousness, there is no conflict. You will act differently because you are completely appropriate to the situation. You face the situation from your completeness, which is choiceless, without direction. There is simply an extension of this completeness into time and space: that is action.

It is important to act according to your understanding. Feel all your surroundings from this point of view, which is not a point of view. Once you have understood the situation, use the power of transposition. When you really understand something, you can transpose it. I would even say that the only proof that you understand is that you can transpose it onto every situation. Otherwise, you have not understood it.

When one is not established in consciousness, does it make sense to act as if one were acting from consciousness?

In any case, as long as you are a human being you live and act in the world. You can perfectly see and know when your action comes from the split mind, when you choose and select. Then you are no longer with the facts. In taking note of this you will be spontaneously brought to the timeless.

I's not so easy to see when I act from the split mind.

You will see afterwards that you have acted through choice. When you have seen it afterwards several times, you will catch it as you do it. The moment you take note, you are out of the process. This is the first step. Then you should knowingly integrate this note-taking, become attuned to it.

Is that fixing on the witness?

No, it's not a fixation. The note-taking, the witness aspect, completely disappears. It exists for a moment and dissolves. So in every action come back to your verticality, the timeless where there is no knower and nothing known.

Seeing happens spontaneously; global understanding appears instantaneously. But is not transposition an art? Does it not call for some qualities like talent, seriousness, even a certain effort?

It depends how the divine plays in you. There's only spontaneous action, right action.

Spontaneous action can never hurt others?

Never. Because it doesn't go through the split mind. It takes no effort to transpose understanding. There are people who have a glimpse of the light but have not integrated the temporal in the light. In a certain way they deny manifestation because they don't understand it is an expression of the light.

In the "stop," there always seems to be the "I" feeling. If there is something in the stop before the "I" feeling, there's no recognition of it radical enough to be realized. When the stop happens, I assume there must be a blank-out because the recognition is of not being in fantasy; but there is still an "I" feeling of being-hereness.

115

In seeing the truth, there is no "I." No one sees the truth. There is only truth. I keep saying this, but it is astonishing when you see that everything you are aware of is only an object, because your real nature is the subject of all objects. What you are looking for is the looker.

I would say you have understood this principle, but don't take your luggage and leave before the understanding is established in the clarity of the mind.

Do you have to learn deep relaxation before this stopping without a stopper can happen?

Yes, relaxation is giving-up in a certain way.

It's not already there in organic memory?

Yes, the total giving-up, the total relaxation is as if you said, "I'm at an end, I've looked everywhere, I don't know."

You can learn to relax your body, but you cannot learn this profound relaxation. It is the result of seeing things as they are that brings you to deep relaxation.

I came here with a wish for something else, with no real sense of giving up anything. Suddenly, there is a sense that the motivation, the wish has been all ego.

There is only a giving-up of what you are not. That is all. You are not the body, senses and mind. You can give all that up. That is all you can do.

You say to live one's understanding as much as possible. Does that mean to bring to each daily situation I encounter as much understanding, as much globality, as I'm able to? Is that transposition, or is it something more spontaneous and non-volitional?

In this transposition, there is no volition. It is absolutely spontaneous.

What can I do with whatever openness or understanding I have now?

Live with it.

To sustain, to nourish it, that sounds like an effort.

There is no effort needed to sustain it. When you really understand it, you love it. You will not go away from it. It is the most precious jewel that you have. You will spontaneously keep it.

A few evenings ago, I felt very caught in a restriction and suddenly it was as if you had said to me, "See the roles that you identify with, they are restrictive for you." I saw these roles as garments. It was as if they had floated away and they were there in front of me. A sense of wonderment and relief came that I could pick up the garments and wear them, but I didn't have to. A thought came: I am not of those. What is the nature of that thought?

When you say, "I am not," that comes from what you are. "I am not" anything, that is body, senses and mind. When you say it really, this comes from what you are. But it must not remain in the mind. Don't even say it; give all your love, your attention to the understanding. In other words, live with it. Every time you are free from earning your living, give your love to what you are. Then there will come a moment when you are the light during the action.

And by "live with it" would it be just remembering the feeling of that moment? Let it be present more?

It is present, we don't need to remember it. It remembers you.

You have to make space for it?

Yes.

How can the looker dissolve itself, since it seems its very nature is hidden?

The moment you see the looker is what he is looking for, then all belongs to the looker. The looker knows itself by itself.

After the last retreat I had a tremendous sense of "I know who I am. I'm not any of those things that I thought I was. I don't need to go looking any

117

more for anything." There was this tremendous openness inside. Then I got all excited about it. I felt like I had discovered a precious jewel; but transposing it, living it, didn't happen sufficiently although many things have not had as much hold on me since then.

This understanding must also dissolve in being the understanding. There is no more excitement. You are completely attuned to being the understanding. Live the understanding. The understanding has been formulated in words. Make it your own. Welcome your own formulation. See that you do not need any other formulation.

But you must come back to the geometrical understanding, the geometrical representation; otherwise, it becomes a kind of mystical experience and this mystical experience is confusion for the mind. It is not clarity for the mind.

So the mind must be much more clear?

Yes. The mind will know what belongs to the mind. The mind sees its limits.

So the geometrical understanding is the mind coming to see its limits?

The geometrical understanding is when the geometrical representation vanishes in its essence. When you see a work of art, the elements are distributed in space and time. But, in a work of art one doesn't emphasize the material. Of course, we look at the material and the presentation, but it gives no hold to us. It disappears and the essence remains. The essence means I love it, it is beauty, I am the beauty.

But the geometrical understanding disappears in the essence, which is the beingness, the stillness. The understanding is a jewel which you must always wear around your neck. Never give it up. Do not give it up and deny it. Do not put it away. Keep it on you. In time it will dissolve in its essence.

Live with it until the representation becomes living understanding. The geometrical understanding must not be an artificial construction of the mind. It must be the result of inquiring. Otherwise, we will find we are able to make a beautiful copy of Manet or other masters, but it remains only a copy. It is by inquiring and exploring life first-hand that we come to being the understanding.

This clarity arises intuitively rather than through some intellectual process. It seems as if there is a leap of intuition, not a process of intellectual discovery?

This intuition must appear in a really clear mind. But the motive, the source of the intuition, must sustain the inquiry. When the source is forgotten, the inquiry has no power. When you explore all your motives and derive that you are looking for happiness or peace or real love, it is important that you refer every situation, every event to it.

That means that you have explored, in a certain way, all your doing and thinking. When you have inquired into all your doing and thinking and can say it is not in this or that direction, you become oriented. There is no more discussion. It is from this moment that you come to the sacred quest.

It feels that with this orientation there is nothing left to do. There is no longer energy for things that aren't in that orientation. They naturally drop away. There is no intellectual effort involved in it. It just takes you.

Yes. It may come out of deep desire. But you know it comes from this desire. The mystic in a certain way is full of desire. He is completely attuned to his desire. And as the desire comes from what you desire, it brings you to the desired. But still the mind may not be clear.

The motive, the professed desire, must be sustained so that you look for the essence of your life. When you have explored all around you and have come to the logical result that you cannot find it in any direction, then there is a giving-up of all directions and you will live in the directionless. There is a stop. There is no more dispersion. All energy comes back to its homeground. It is a moment of not-knowing.

*W*HEN YOU SAY TO INHALE AND WAIT *until the body gives the order to exhale, do we hold our breath or is it just a matter of not doing anything with it, letting it be?*

First look at the quality of the exhalation, because these muscles are more or less the same as for the inhalation; but in the exhalation you can more easily feel all the intercostal muscles which bind the ribs and which are necessary for inhalation-exhalation. So when the exhalation is completely equal, the same intensity, when you feel there is no jump (jerkiness), then you can better explore the inhalation.

In the inhalation, as in the exhalation, there must be no intention. If there is any intention you use force. You should simply be open for the inhalation. When you have inhaled, keep the air comfortably and feel yourself completely expanded in space. Then offer the exhalation to the space in front of you. Wait until the exhalation is completely accomplished. Sometimes, when there is fear and anxiety, the exhalation does not come to the end. So consciously come to the end of the breath and then you will feel that pure energy remains. It takes time to eliminate the pure energy, so that you really die in silence. Then wait for the inner need to inhale. You will find that you become more and more comfortable in this waiting, this giving up the breath after exhalation.

121

This interval between exhalation and inhalation is the timeless reality. Inhalation-exhalation is only a superimposition on this reality. So the interval between exhalation and inhalation is not an absence of breathing. It is the presence of your real being. You will become more and more attuned to this interval and something astonishing will occur—you feel an identity with this reality. It is the background to the activity, the exhalation-inhalation. You can use the breathing process in two ways: when you emphasize the energy body in itself; then of course there are various ways to awaken the energy through breathing. But what we do here has a more spiritual purpose, that is why I emphasize so much the interval between inhalation-exhalation and especially exhalation-inhalation.

So be very careful not to push the air. There must be none of our habitual anticipation of a finality to the exhalation and inhalation. There is no grasping and no forcing the air to come to an end. When you are attentive from moment to moment you will see that there is a certain difficulty in letting the air flow smoothly because your muscles are not very conscious and the air flows in jumps. The breath should be absolutely equal, equal in the same way as when you direct your breath towards the flame of a candle; and the angle, the inclination of the flame, remains constantly the same. This is a guarantee that your exhalation is directed equally. But you can feel, you can hear when your breath is moving equally and evenly on its own. And then you will see the effect on the psychosomatic body. Thinking becomes quieter, there is a kind of equanimity in your body, and there is also a certain pleasure in right breathing.

What is the significance of hearing a sound in the left ear? Kind of a high sound or a flute sound.

Before the world is created, first is sound. And virtually, potentially, all that is created is in this sound. You can hear it in a certain way when your body is very purified. And it appears in the right ear. We call it *nada*.

In the right ear?

Yes, in the right ear, not in the left, in the right ear.

Why is nada *in the right ear?*

Unfortunately I cannot tell you. (laughter) When the psycho-somatic body is completely relaxed and all the different levels, layers, come to a giving-up, then there is this slight vibration. But this is an object like any other. It belongs to the accumulation of knowledge.

Going back to breathing, in breathing out here, there is a strong contraction which resists breathing out . . .

Yes.

So I can't go all the way unless I force it. It just freezes the whole body. Do I just watch it and sooner or later it just gives way, or is it just one of these things that is a part of the anatomy?

Begin feeling first the abdominal region, like a tire around you. Feel it first localized in front, then left and right and behind. When you can really localize it, feel the tire; then you breathe only in the abdominal region. When you have mastered it, you move up here to the intercostal region. You again feel the tire around you as you inhale, in front, left, right and behind, like a wheel. When you have really felt it, mastered it, then you go up to the collarbones. So when you have really mastered the three levels, then again inhale. The inhalation is accomplished in the abdominal, then the intercostal, then the cervical. The exhalation goes cervical, intercostal, abdominal.

Every breath starts here?

Exactly, you start here. It is like a flame, here . . . second . . . third . . . you stop it . . . you exhale . . . Like putting water in a bottle. The fact that you have still some difficulty here means that these muscles, the muscles which bind the ribs together, are not really articulated, not really conscious. So I would say go back for some time to articulating the three levels: the first level, second level, third level, exhale, upper part, middle part, lower part. The body will become more conscious; and, when you have mastered it and it occurs naturally and normally, then you are in possession of the space. That means you are no longer fixed to the levels, but the in-breathing and out-breathing occur in the space.

So the breathing movement goes from here to here?

Yes. But eventually you emphasize only the space. The in-breathing and out-breathing all happen in the space. In the beginning, you visualize the space in front of you, on the left, right and behind; but later you give up the visualization. You can never at the same time visualize in front, behind, left and right. So to feel the global space you must go away from all visualization. Because you can only *feel* globality, you can never represent it. Then the breath is just like a flame. (long pause) You are completely one with it. It is a pure perception. There is no thinking in it. There is no concept. You are completely one with the flowing of the breath.

Well, I still get mixed up between going in and out.

Only become conscious of the three levels.

And since it is so unnatural I have to be really . . .?

It is natural. It is really physiological. It has, strictly speaking, nothing to do with the system of pranayama. It is simply normal function, physically, even medically correct, I would say. Our body is made up in this way.

So the body naturally goes into this rhythm if it is given a chance?

Absolutely, yes. Look at how very small babies breathe before their bodies are conditioned and contracted. When you become more and more conscious of all the muscles you will find that your exhalation is naturally much longer. The inhalation is still a little shorter but the exhalation is quite long. The breathing is really exclusively through the nostrils; don't combine it with breathing through the mouth.

Both nostrils? Usually one nostril is clogged.

Yes, then you must see why it is closed.

Food?

Yes, it is certainly your program of food. For you, butter, poison; cheese, poison . . . And then also those very good minestrone, vegetables cooked in very little water; these soups are too concentrated, too rich in mineral salts. They affect the sinuses. So when you wake up in the morning and you have eaten this kind of food, you will see your nostrils are obstructed. If you correct your diet, you will see that you wake up and there is no problem.

If you like minestrone, cook the vegetables in two waters and make the soup with the second water, not the first water. If the nostrils are still obstructed you should do the face bath. You put in your basin water as hot as you can stand, then you inhale, and then put your whole face in the water.

Do you inhale the water?

No, just immerse the face. Do it six, eight, even nine times. And then put cold water in the basin and do the same. After five or six days all kinds of residues will be eliminated. So you have all the secrets now!

In living the understanding, but before being established in it, there is a going away from it into the object, becoming identified with the object. You used a term, I can't remember your exact words, but you said there is a way in which you can find yourself back to it. I know you were not giving a technique. Perhaps you were again talking about organic memory finding you and bringing you back. Is there a subtlety here you can bring out?

Every object is projected from you and has its homeground in you. Potentially, then, the object seen can bring you to pure seeing, an object heard can bring you to pure hearing. In this hearing and seeing there is nobody who sees or hears and no object seen or heard. There is only hearing, there is only seeing. It is not in subject-object relationship. It is completely non-dual. This is the shortest way taught in the direct approach.

When you come to the understanding that you are not the psychosomatic body, in this moment you have a glimpse of what you are. But you can never have a glimpse of what you are when it is simply a question from the mind. The question "Who am I?" does not come from the mind. Asking "Who am I?" is accompanied by a tremendous energy; you are on fire. I think you can compare it to the condensed energy present when you are very angry or completely joyful. I would say this kind of energy *must* be there to ask the questions: Who am I?, What am I?, What is life? Then you have a glimpse of what you are. It is important that you have the glimpse for this is the understanding of the right perspective. Then you live with the right perspective. There is less and less dispersion. Your life becomes more and more oriented. You use all your energy in a completely different way. As your life becomes more oriented you see things differently. Before, you saw things only from the point of view of the "I," the "me." When you see things from the point of view of the "I" or the "me," you live mechanically, in choice, in selection. You may say, "I see it," but you don't really see it, because your seeing is colored by selection, selection for security, for pleasure, to avoid, and so on.

When you have a glimpse of reality it is already in a certain way in your background. You see things less and less personally; there comes the quality of global vision, where there is no choice, no selection. You see things more and more as they are, not as you wish them to be, but as they really are. You live in this perspective, you love it; it is a jewel you wear, maybe several times a day. Then there comes a moment in your life that even this geometrical representation, the perspective, dissolves in your real nature. And then there is no return. This switch-over is absolutely sudden, instantaneous. You live now without anticipation, without end-gaining. You live absolutely in the now. Thinking is a practical, useful tool which you use when you need it, but you no longer think when there is no need to think. There is no more daydreaming. You enjoy real freedom from thought. Oh, you will become a happy man! What more do you want?

Is it possible to say, sir, what brings that about? That sudden change?

You come to this point through inquiring. You undertake inquiring when there is discrimination, discernment. But the ego cannot discern; discerning comes from discernment itself, the insight that you are not the psychosomatic body. To inquire about life calls for a serious character; it takes a profound seriousness. Be earnest! But I don't think it should be a problem for you to be earnest.

(long pause)

I see you here for the second time. I love you. Have you a question?

I had a question yesterday.

And today?

It is the same question, the one I didn't ask yesterday. When I wake up sometimes the very first thing I wake with is fear.

Be completely aware when you say there is fear. When you are alert the question naturally arises: Who has fear? Who is afraid? You have my guarantee that when you ask who has fear, the next day you will see before the fear appears that the "I," the "me," which you take yourself to be, is put in relation to certain circumstances in your daily life. The ego saw the circumstance and felt no security, so there is fear, there is anticipation. So first face the fear, face the sensation "fear." You will see that you, the knower of the fear, are not afraid, that only an object has fear. But don't push it away, face it completely, explore it in every corner. It is localized in your body somewhere.

When you ask the question, "Who has fear?," you will see that the body wakes in the morning in freedom, but immediately you identify with the old representation of yourself. You put yourself in relation to some activity that you have projected. Remember that the personality who has fear is an object, and the situation which produced the fear is an object too. So now there is a relation from object to object. The moment you see this you are out of the cage. Don't try to manipulate, touch or interfere because all this belongs to the cage and you remain in a vicious circle. You cannot reason your way out of the problem, only see that you are the knower of the problem and not the problem. When you are still, with your real self, there is no fear.

Be careful also how you go to sleep. Don't take all your problems to sleep. There is a kind of hygiene in going to sleep and in waking up. Systematically lay your problems at the front door when you go to sleep.

Sir, I assume that what you just described about investigating the fear is a good example of inquiry, and I am wondering if there are any other ways of inquiring you could tell us about or if we must come to inquire each in our own way?

The first step is to face, become aware of, the mass of agitation, contraction, which you call fear. The name that you immediately give to the sensation you feel is not the actual fear. The word fear is memory, the word fear does not belong to the actual sensation; so free yourself from the concept fear and face only the perception. Then automatically you will know how to observe it, how to look at it with love and compassion. In this looking you don't give any food to the concept fear and an energy wakes up and integrates in your wholeness. So begin by asking, "Who has fear?" and then you will come more and more to know the mechanism. There are people who wake up every morning with fear, afraid of facing work, facing the boss, facing the news from the bank and so on. It is constant anticipation. But who has fear? It is absolutely indispensable, absolutely necessary to seriously ask this question. And live with the question.

And that applies regardless of what the object is, even "Who has joy?," for example?

Yes. Look again at the situation which apparently made you afraid, look again. But as long as we are an independent entity we are constantly vulnerable to fear.

So the question brings a return to the silence.

Absolutely.

Jung talked about what he called the unconscious; he also talked about the archetypes. So, for example, with fear, I wonder if, sometimes, certain fears just don't have any apparent cause; and from the Jungian point of view they might be an archetypal energy that is appearing unconsciously. Or there might be unconscious conflicts that we aren't aware of so we can't so easily set aside the concept, you know, see through what is causing the fear because it really is deeply unconscious. What do you think of that point of view and how does one work with so-called unconscious material?

This is a theoretical point of view, but I am saying that when you really face the sensation it will bring you to the threshold of the origin of fear. It takes time to face the deep levels of what we call fear, anxiety. Even when you are established in your real nature the elimination of all the physiological residues takes time. The patterns from childhood are very strong.

So, ultimately, the sensations are like the gate, you might say, the entry-way into what is often called the unconscious. But it is an entry-way that will ultimately bring us to the source of fear and also the release of fear.

You may have faced certain situations in your life and you saw certain elements. Actually there were far more elements to the situation than you saw, and these elements which you did not see, saw you.

I'm not certain what you mean.

129

A situation is composed of many elements. You may immediately grasp three or four elements and come to the conclusion that you "see the situation." And this situation which is composed of only three or four elements of information produces fear in you. When you really face the sensation and you visualize, recreate the situation again, you will be astonished to observe that many points come up which you had not seen before but which saw you. These new elements establish a completely new situation. You have a completely new vision of the situation.

In other words, our fear is often based on seeing a very partial limited view of the situation and when we see the situation completely and fully the fear dissolves.

Yes, yes. We are always grasping certain points too quickly out of the need for security.

There is such a thing as fear of the creator and that seems like it's necessary or desirable. Is that so?

Do you think fear can be creative?

No, the fear of the creator.

But according to you, who is the creator of the fear, the fear of disappearing, psychological survival?

That fear I am speaking of seems to me to be part of the essence of the universe, one of the essential qualities. It just is; so I perceive it, I accept it, I take it on, I create it. In that sense I bring it into myself. I accept it.

You are talking of a god who creates fear. I don't see it in this way. God is absolute perfection. There is nothing to perfect, for it is pure beauty. Only love can awaken us, not fear. You should investigate more. In my opinion, you have identified yourself with secondhand information. Don't live with secondhand information. Don't live with beliefs. You have the capacity to explore and really find out what actually is. You don't have to accept a fear-inspiring god.

After the instantaneous awakening, and while the body-mind is reorchestrating, is there a forgetfulness or identification that comes in or is it simply witnessed with total clarity?

The old pattern has no more role to play and automatically there is a kind of elimination. You still remain in conditioning but the superficial conditionings are certainly eliminated. However, we are conditioned by our language very strongly and heredity—that you are a man and not a woman—this also is conditioning. You are, in a certain way, the result of your father and your mother; heredity goes on. But you are not your conditioning. You are the Self.

In the Sunday morning session you asked us to feel the left brain, then to feel the right brain, then to feel the neck and then you said to be aware of the space where the three meet. If I recall rightly some years ago you once said that the awakening of consciousness comes from the back. I inferred the back of the head. Could you say something on this place where we put our head on our pillow every night?

The factory for producing thoughts is in the brain, so I think that first we must come to the relaxed brain, left and right side. When we listen to the brain there is a very deep letting-go in our organism. We feel the left and right brain like sponges, opening and closing, opening and closing, a constant vibration. When you come to the absolutely relaxed state this movement is much more subtle, a little closing and a little opening. Then with the help of your visualization you can link your brain to the old brain in your neck. When you are located in the region of the old brain, you will feel a certain non-directed energy, a pulsation which does not manifest in specific thoughts and desires. For a certain time you remain with this pulsation of energy in which thoughts and desires have no more possibility of striking the brain. Then there is the giving-up of this non-directed energy also, and you find yourself in the heart region, in the center. In the center you are free from space and time.

As long as you are localized in your head you are visited by thoughts, constantly coming and going. For example, in our morning meditation when we go into the space in front of us, then everywhere, there is a kind of dilation, expansion. In this expansion the brain has no more role to play. But as long as you localize yourself in the brain you can never stop thinking, it goes on and on. You must go away from this factory.

Where time meets the timeless is in the heart. Time can never *reach* the timeless. Time can only *meet* the timeless in the now, in the moment itself; it is the only moment. Truth can only be understood by truth. The timeless can only be understood by the timeless. So time meets the timeless in the heart.

I wanted to ask you something about the heart. What I find generally in life is that it closes and there is just no space for the timeless or the jewel to be there. I just wondered if there is something that you could say that would help me to keep it open?

The only way to be open is when you admire and you love. Loving and admiring opens your heart. But I think your feeling of being compressed, closed here, may be purely physiological. In deep relaxation and in breathing, become aware of this important region. It will help you. It is, I am sure, not a psychological problem; it is more physiological.

This area between the eyes seems sometimes to be energized or activated. It does not seem to be necessarily connected to thinking, it is more visual somehow. I just wonder, when you say to go away from the forehead, what about this energy center?

I would say first feel the forehead, even go to the eyes; free the eyes from taking, grasping. The only way to free your eyes is to feel your eyes. Feel the eyes are living, feel the convexity, visualize them as very large. Relax your eyes in this way so that you see them several inches in front of you. Completely relax. Then your forehead feels like a curtain. You must feel it is a curtain that covers your face completely, like an Islamic woman. Then will come deep relaxation.

There are many traditions and many psychologies, many approaches to the body and the psyche: the Tibetan tradition, the Indian tradition, the

Christian, Judaic. We all come with conditioning and interests related to those different traditions. I was thinking, for example, of having worked for some time trying to be in touch with the hara, *the part around the navel. But all of these techniques in a way seem like manipulation. In deep relaxation, in letting-go with sensation, these energy centers are touched naturally. Yet it is as though I and others very often try to approach them from the outside, trying to manipulate these energy centers and saying this one or that one is more important. In a way, the teaching you are bringing seems to cut through all of that, because it has to do with a letting-go of ideas, of concepts, of images. Yet that letting-go is so difficult. We hear it intellectually, we hear the words and we want to embody them somehow, in some part of the body or the whole body. I feel a hint of the perspective you are talking about and yet I see myself wanting to begin to manipulate it again. It comes in from all quarters. Maybe someone tells me that if I relax this or that it will help, or if I breathe like this it will help, etc. It is difficult for me to ask this question, but the pure way of doing nothing seems so difficult and so high; yet the way through the body seems just filled with all kinds of possibilities of manipulation and illusion.*

You refer to various traditions. People today keep certain traditional formulations which were formulated hundreds and thousands of years ago. The formulation of this tradition was according to the understanding, the level of the society at the time. This formulation of a tradition is the doctrine. It belongs to the traditional aspect. Tradition, as I see it, means that which is truth, that which is transmitted. That means the truth transmits the truth. You can never transmit the doctrine. The doctrine is formulated every twenty or fifty years. You could even say the doctrine appears from moment to moment. So tradition means what is transmitted. The truth is transmitted. Ideas, doctrine can never bring transmutation. It is only the truth that is transmitted which can bring transmutation of the psychosomatic body. The psychosomatic body on its own can never transform itself. It is only consciousness, truth, which can transform it. So in any religious teaching there is an exoteric part, the traditional, and an esoteric part, the Tradition. The exoteric part is very conventional and is not really the essence of the teaching. The essence of the teaching is esoteric. The interpretation on the esoteric level of every tradition, Judaism, Christianity, Taoism, and so on, is the only truth. There are not several truths, there is only truth. Truth can never be objectified, can never be perceived. You can only be it. Truth can only be transmitted through truth. Transmutation can only take place through our real nature, our real nature which knows itself by itself, and doesn't need an agent.

I FEEL I MUST FIND A TEACHER WHO HAS ATTAINED THE SELF, *a teacher or guru who is enlightened. I would like to know what your opinion is of this. Also, can you tell me, are you yourself such a teacher?*

First let me make it clear for you that there is nobody to become enlightened. You must see it very clearly, that there is no one who is enlightened. When you are still, welcoming all that appears, potentially you are enlightened.

Be completely attuned to the silent moment where there is nobody who is silent and nothing is silent, there is only silence.

Faced with the prospect of going back into the world, into so-called normal life, I have the idea based on reading and maybe intuition that I don't exist nor does anybody else exist and relationship is just meaningless. There is a feeling . . . (the questioner rambles on)

The question is?

The question is, what to do? Going back into the world seems to involve doing and, of course, there is ultimately nothing to do. I am in a quandary because I have spent so much energy and many years of effort trying to change, then I read in your book that all change is just like moving the furniture around. When I go back, people will ask me what I got out of the

seminar and I'll tell them I certainly got my money's worth, but I can't
say how. It is a paradox, it is something that is unclear to me . . .

Now give me the real question because until now you are saying
things that belong to a confused mind. What really is your question?

The question is, who am I?

Ahh! Ask the question really, seriously, earnestly. To ask this question you must be worthy to become the answer, to be the answer.
And this question can never be asked by the mind. When you ask
the question at the right moment, then you are the answer. So *be*
the answer. Be the answer.

Yes . . . There is nothing else.

Nothing else. Already too much!

Would you talk about the relationship between the witness awareness and
consciousness?

As long as you take yourself for somebody you are the witness.
When you clearly see that this somebody is only a thought-construct, then the reflex to take yourself for somebody is completely
eliminated along with the witness. Then there is only consciousness. Consciousness is the witness and the witness is consciousness. The witness is not a function, but remains a function as long
as you are a doer, a thinker.

When you ask the question see really that the question is the
answer. There is no answer without a question and no question
without an answer. The seeker is the sought and the sought is the
seeker, for there are not two but only one. So when you ask the
question for yourself, live with the question. It is the question
which reveals the answer. You are the living answer. But you can
never objectify the answer; it can never be an object. What you are
fundamentally, you can never know it, you can only be it. In this

waiting without waiting, you are totally yourself, present. That is a non-state of being open constantly, and a constant welcoming.

Could you please satisfy my curiosity and tell me whether turiya *is a state or a non-state?*

As long as you are not established in *turiya* it is a state, a fourth state. But the moment you are awake in *turiya*, in *turiyacitta*, then it is no longer a state. It is the non-state.

So at that point it is the same as the word you use which I think is sahaja.

Yes, *sahaja* is not a state. In a state you go in and you go out. *Sahaja* always is.

I found myself overwhelmed by the idea of geometrical representation which you spoke about the other day. How would one begin to approach understanding this?

You know that all that you perceive is an object perceived in time and space and an object exists because there is a subject. You know you are the subject, the subject of all objects, but you don't see clearly yet that this subject can never be an object, can never be perceived. So there is a picture, a representation, of an object needing a subject to be perceived and a subject which can never be perceived. So this logical understanding, this representation shows you that, in order to know the subject, there is nothing to attain or obtain, or to grasp, because all that you grasp or that you attain or achieve is perceivable and therefore can only be an object. Knowing the subject belongs to a completely new kind of knowledge. So the mind sees its limits and gives up. Then you no longer live in thought but in a kind of fore-feeling which is at the threshold of an insight. So live with this representation of an unthinkable subject which you are. Live with it until there is a moment when it dissolves completely and you are it. That is an instantaneous awakening of yourself, what you are, the ultimate subject.

It is something tremendous when you clearly feel that there is nothing to attain, nothing to obtain; when you feel that every step you undertake is a going away because what you are fundamentally is too near to step towards. Then see how this understanding acts on you. Feel how it produces a total giving-up, a letting-go on all levels the moment you feel yourself in complete absence of any representation. In this absence of trying to reprepresent the "I," there is true presence where nobody is present and present to nothing; there is only presence. Then the world and your surroundings appear completely differently, because you see your surroundings from your totality, from your globality. You live freely in the now, without end-gaining, without anticipation, all your energy in the present, not in a becoming process. But for you, because you have a strong component of feeling, it may be enough that when you are really still, when you have moments of stillness, you are completely attuned to these moments, then there is an unfolding. Let yourself be solicited in these moments. This is another way in which you can see that the looker is what he is looking for.

You said that it is tremendous to understand that there is nothing to become. Is there a desire to sing and to laugh, or is there just being quiet?

I use the word "tremendous" because it is an earthquake. All that you believe, all that you have accepted as secondhand information, everything you have read in books, all your experiences—in this bazaar that you live in—explodes.

When you began your quest for the Self did you have the certainty that you would come to know that Self?

The certainty comes from the certainty.

I know for example that in the desire to obtain a certain object, the desire itself, the wanting and the earnestness in wanting it, somehow brings it about.

The desire comes from what you desire, for otherwise there would be no desire. So really live with your desire. But to know your real desire needs maturity because your real desire is oriented, it is the Desire of all desires. When there is right discrimination, right discernment, you know that this desire comes from what you ultimately long for. Then live with it; be earnest. In living with it earnestly there is no longer dispersion. Give all your intelligence, all your heart to this desire. You can be sure that one day this desire is fulfilled because it is your nearest. It is nearer than stroking your cat.

Could you speak about why progressive practice, which I and some of the people here have studied, even though it can lead to an unconditioned state, doesn't seem to lead to the non-state of permanent awakening?

In the background of the path of progression is the idea that there is something to obtain, something to achieve. You go through many purifications, abstinences, observances, body postures, pranayama, dhyana, samadhi. You go through all these kinds of states, all kinds of purifications, but all this happens in subject-object relationship. Just suppose you come one day to the point when there is nothing left to purify. You still remain in subject-object relationship because the absence of an object, purified object, is still an object. By then you are very strongly conditioned. So don't waste your time and energy. You now know that truth can only be found by truth. You know that you can never find truth by untruth and that the mind is untruth. The mind can know all the workings of the mind but can never go beyond the mind. So in all these progressive approaches you remain in some realm of the mind. In the direct approach the target is directly to the heart, not the mind.

Listen only to the teaching which shows you, in a clear peda-gogical way, that there is nothing to be obtained. Then naturally you'll become free from all this stuff that you think you can obtain and one day you will see the flame that you are. When you listen to the saying that there is nothing to obtain, that only truth can know the truth, automatically all that is untruth gives itself up and you find yourself in listening. You find yourself living in an abso-lute giving-up, a complete letting-go. I would say it is a non-state where you will have the glimpse, where you are at the threshold of what you are fundamentally.

When you spoke of explosion I suddenly had a sense that it can't be understood by the mind, because it comes from something tremendously vaster, more like the universe of the heart, some kind of tremendous upsurging.

The earthquake, the tremendous, isn't the mind. It is not only a vertically moving, it is also a laterally moving earthquake.

What connection is there, if any, between emotion, which is negative or positive, and the heart which you have been talking about where the vertical and horizontal meet? I have had many moments of experiencing that every posture can be a yogic posture in a sense. It is a kind of expansion that takes place momentarily, then there's a kind of excitement and then there is a whole flood of thoughts like: what does this mean? is it this? how am I going to talk about it? how will I ask him about it? But there are emotions that come up too, and sometimes the emotion is one of wonderment—but it has still got that taste of being very much caught up in time, very much caught in emotivity. So what is the connection between emotion and heart, because I think it is important to be clear about this so that the mind doesn't weave more stories about it?

I think that what you experience sometimes is more a kind of wonder, a kind of astonishment to feel yourself at certain moments in the timeless, simply being witness to what you do, being free from it. It is in you but you are completely free of it. I would not qualify these glimpses as reactions of the "I," the "me," which is in the category of emotivity. I think these moments belong to the timeless. In emotivity, you are bound to the moment, you are bound to the situation.

When you become more and more familiar with your attention, attention without tension, attention without intention, it will grow in welcoming and waiting and openness, in living and waiting without waiting for anything. In waiting without waiting for something, in welcoming, you are free from any thought construct. You are simply open. All your surroundings refer to this openness, because you can never find yourself in any object. You can only find yourself in openness. In openness you can never assert your being and never localize it. But we are so accustomed to states, and in states there are subject-object relationships. We would automatically like to see ourselves also as an object, to think of ourselves as an ideal Mr. Smith or Mr. Durant. We would like to wake up one morning and say, "I am now the perfect, the enlightened, Mr. Smith." But all this is a concept. We are nothing but openness; we are a total absence, yet in this openness and this absence there is the "I am."

It feels as though I can produce a state of openness, like the feeling of space when we are doing the body-work. It seems as if it's just another state. But you are saying that we are not a state.

No, you cannot produce your natural non-state, but you can have a very good analogy. When you close your eyes and visualize immensity, space around you, and the body sensation dissolves, your seeing, feeling, smelling, touching go completely into this space, dissolve in space. Then there is a touch of freedom. It is only a kind of analogy, but it is a very beautiful analogy.

I don't know exactly how to describe this but I sort of feel that I had an experience of that. So I try to, you know, continue that through the day, but then I get hypersensitive and anything that is not expansion feels like pain. It is sort of making me nuts.

But you identify yourself with your pain. Instead, ask by whom is this pain perceived and who is the perceiver? Don't try to get an answer immediately, but go around it. It is perceived in the body. Who is the perceiver? I'm not asking you the question, I'm telling you only to ask yourself.

Also you said that when you reach an awakening you go through a process of elimination.

Yes. The elimination before awakening comes from higher reasoning—*vidyavritti*. After awakening, it comes from knowledge.

I was wondering, can you go through a process of elimination before you awaken? Is there any elimination you can do before you awaken that has any value?

There are certain eliminations before you are really in your real state. As the body rights itself there is elimination. When you understand what is right food, what is really food, there is elimination. There is elimination on many levels.

A complete elimination of the conditioning of the body, deep body memories and conditionings?

Certain conditioning will go, superficial conditioning will go; but there is conditioning which comes through heredity which may never go. But you are not your body. If you are a woman, you will remain a woman; you will not become an angel. A woman is already a conditioning. And be happy to be a woman! I think the angel may be waiting to be one too!

All my questions seem to be a deviation from the central theme. But I was just interested in what you were saying about right food and right eating. Is it the same for everybody or how does it work?

You are a result of food. You are a food product. The sun, the air, heat, what you take through your mouth and so on, you are really the result of what you have absorbed. When you wake up in the morning and your body is heavy, you feel your body very conditioned, not really disposed to face the day; then you may question your body. You may question how you lived yesterday, what kind of newspaper you read, what kind of meal you ate. You may see that you ate a certain kind of food which has not been properly digested. You will inquire until one day you find what we call real food, food that is still alive, and a right combination of food. You will see that certain things are digested in your mouth, certain things in your stomach, certain things in your intestine. You will inquire and you will experiment until you wake up one day and feel refreshed, completely lucid, awakened. Then that means that you are eating right food in the right climate. Maybe you should move from Amsterdam and come here to San Francisco or vice versa. Seeing how what you absorb acts on you is very important.

Are we, through welcoming our environment, able to reduce what we don't want to absorb?

Yes, you will make a choice, what to eat, what to absorb. You will make a choice, a kind of selection, a kind of discrimination. You may no longer drink good cognac in the morning. A good cognac in the morning may be very nice, but you will not want to drink it. Very good black coffee . . . you may no longer drink it. You make a selection. You may no longer see certain people or attend certain functions or read certain books. You will want to hear good music, not bad music. You will look at good painting, not poor painting. There comes a selection. You will live in a well-proportioned room and so on. All your surroundings act on you, the room where you live, the direction of your bed, the people you frequent, all . . . because you are the result of what you absorb. You have already made a certain selection, otherwise you would not be here.

This is something that I don't understand. All objects point back to who I am, so what difference does it make whether the object is cognac and coffee or whether it is wheatgrass? It is essentially the same.

Absolutely. (laughter)

Essentially it is the same, so all that will be different is that the appearance will change. Some saints and teachers smoked their whole lives and they got cancer, but apparently they were clear in some way. So it is just some question that I don't understand about the importance of . . .

When your body is not pure, the higher reasoning is affected. There are objects which simply do not go together. Certain bodies don't go with cognac. So there is an intelligent selection. What is the relationship between objects? You know that every object has its potentiality in you, you as the ultimate subject. Your body is an object.

So the object is affected by what it takes in?

All that is perceived is an object. It has its reality only because you are the ultimate subject, otherwise it doesn't exist. Where is it in deep sleep?

Exactly, so the subject is not affected. In deep sleep I am not affected.

No, not at all, you are in your glory!

But is the subject affected by the choice between coffee or wheatgrass?

No, no, never. It is only one object that affects another object when they don't go together. Even an object that is good for some may be bad for another. There are people who drink a good cognac every morning and are apparently in good shape. I know certain countries where the people drink a very good Schnapps in the morning with black coffee, really quite nice. (laughter)

A moment ago you were talking about something more than good health. You said that one would wake up lucid and light. You are not talking essentially about good health. I mean obviously a lot of people can drink cognac every morning and be in perfect health, but will they have a lucid, light, transparent body?

It depends with what object you go to sleep. (laughter) It depends whether you go into deep sleep with an object or completely objectless. If you are looking to wake up in your real nature you must go to sleep objectless, really in your nakedness. Then your body-mind wakes up differently. It will wake up in the same objectlessness.

But the television you watch in the evening, and the food you absorbed before going to sleep, you will find them still with you in the morning. So, when you see the facts and how these facts act on you, there is a kind of discrimination. Then you make a selection. It is not arbitrary, it is completely normal. It is a selection based on taking your body as a fact, as an object you are not identified with.

So remember, you wake up in the way that belongs to what you have absorbed the previous day.

So we could drink cognac every day of our life and live to be a hundred but wake up every morning in our conditioning perhaps.

Simply take note how you wake up in the morning, it is very clear.

You won't give us any rules? You want us to observe how we wake up?

Exactly, exactly. There are facts: "I am depressed. I don't want to face the day. I feel heavy in my body." Discrimination comes when you accept the facts as they are. I think your body is your nearest object.

I just want to ask one other question. I think it is probably dragging the conversation down a bit, but I just want to ask it once and for all. What about substances like marijuana? People say that twenty years ago you very strongly told people not to take any kind of drug and now you have softened and never say anything about it, so there is a lot of doubt about it. Would you just simply say that people should do what they want and just observe how they wake up in the morning, the same as with the food?

I would say marijuana is not food. That is certain. And you would give it up spontaneously when you really take your body seriously as an object, as a fact. That is certain.

Nisargadatta smoked bidis all his life.

Pardon?

Nisargadatta, he smoked bidis all his life; he never gave them up.

It gives up itself because you see it doesn't appear in your body in a convenient way. You will give it up.

Yes. Nisargadatta stopped smoking in the last year.

One must see it for oneself. When I was young and someone said to me, "Don't do it," then I did exactly the opposite. I didn't like people telling me, "You must, you must not." (laughter) I think when you see it very clearly for yourself then it is right upgiving, not giving-up, upgiving.

When I go back into my daily world after these retreats, I feel that, as the mind gets more active, there is a sense of separation or a returning sense of individuality. Is simply the seeing of that, is this alone the freedom from that sense of individuality?

You can never have a right relation to the world when you start with the world, because then you start from the object. You can only be right with the world when you take the highest stand, that means from consciousness. When you see it from consciousness, the world goes aright. When you approach it from the level of your personality, it cannot help you because your personality belongs to the world. You can never change the world by the world.

When the body-mind wakes up in the morning, let your stand be in consciousness and beingness. You can easily do this in certain moments, you can knowingly go in this openness, in this welcoming, in this acceptance. See all appearings during the morning and afternoon, in this welcoming, in this acceptance. Take note how these things act in you, how they appear to you in this welcoming.

Thank you.

*Y*OU TALKED ABOUT FINDING ONESELF BEHIND. *And you talked in the past about the back of the neck. Is this where the sense of being in awareness is?*

Your real being is not localized anywhere. But localizing yourself behind you frees you from the thought process which occurs mainly in the forehead. When you are behind, you feel the pulsation of the energy but it does not come to formulation. Awareness can never be an object.

It's almost like this "behind" feeling is right before awareness.

Yes, you are free from thought-construct, that is, directed attention. It frees attention to be multidimensional.

Does this non-directional attention bring you to full expansion?

Yes, but don't advertise this, because finding yourself behind is a transition. Hear it, take note of it and forget it. It is a kind of crutch.

When we live in our forehead, there is anticipation, daydreaming, end-gaining, strategy, and so on. In daydreaming you use enormous energy, and anticipation is, in a certain way, daydreaming.

But isn't anticipation a necessity sometimes in daily life? It's not always daydreaming. For example, we need to anticipate when driving a car.

When driving a car you must be totally present to the situation. In car-driving, nobody drives, there is only driving. When you drive your car, you are not in your car. This is a very interesting observation. You are everywhere, there where you look, with your whole body, I would say. That gives you a certain plasticity in driving your car. Then you are open to all the possibilities that could arise. But if you are not completely present, if you are daydreaming, you will not see all the possibilities, the whole picture. Then you will have an accident.

You're not driving your car, you're driving the universe. (laughter)

When we place ourselves behind in the old brain and the thinking process is no longer stimulated, isn't there a drowsiness that initially tends to set in because we are so used to the brain oscillating back and forth with thought and all sorts of impulses? So is there not a kind of slowness, drowsiness, that has to be traversed?

The brain becomes very relaxed, but in this relaxation is tremendous alertness. You become drowsy because you fix the localization behind. But this localization must be integrated in awareness, in presence.

The moment you are no longer in psychological memory, then the brain is open for all possibilities. You are no longer only open to your memory, which is merely for psychological survival. In this autonomy, there is no more memory. The brain functions in a different way when you no longer live in psychological time. When you live in your wholeness, your globality, there is a spontaneous rectification produced by the brain itself.

But the difficulty is that the brain falls into drowsiness because it is accustomed to stimulation and there is a certain clarity needed to maintain continuity and not fall asleep. The same thing happens in meditation, but it doesn't happen so much in waking life when one finds oneself behind. Then it seems to be less of a problem.

You know yourself only in relation to an object, so you make an object of the relaxed brain. It does not appear in your awareness. You become sleepy because you identify with the object and the object does not come alive in you. Let go of all localization, all fixation, all subject-object relationship. Bring back the known to the knowing. You know that the knowing can never be known. Establish yourself in this not-knowing.

This awareness doesn't come from the brain, does it?

Awareness goes through the brain, expresses itself through the brain, but awareness is not in the brain. The brain is in awareness.

The brain is just a tool which is perceived like all tools.

Absolutely. In reality the brain is a sense organ.

So in terms of transmission, there isn't a transmission as the word is normally thought about, but there is a stimulation.

Yes.

So when the energy is collected at the old brain, when one finds oneself behind and the brain slows down, then, since the transmission is so subtle, the stimulation which is always there is now registered.

Transmission is only possible when there is no localization at all, in the total absence of yourself. Only when you are free from the subject-object relationship can there be transmission. Only in this emptiness of the "I" and the "you" can you be stimulated by the silence of another.

It almost feels like a resonance. Like there is a way in which the vibrations come into the same resonance. Instead of stimulation, it's more like a. . .

Yes . . . yes. One must be careful with the word stimulation. One uses the word only for an analogy. When you look at a child's eyes and face and there are still moments in the child when there is complete innocence, purity, and your look is really unconditioned, without memory, I would say there is a kind of echo in you of your own innocence. This may be a little closer to what we mean here by transmission.

It's because it's not something that you lack. It is something that is in you also.

Yes. It is you. It is an awakening in your own self.

Normally in the morning I don't know I'm awake until I'm thinking.

When you start thinking you are awake in the objects and you only know yourself in objects. It depends how you go to sleep, how you give up before sleeping.

It seems there is a critical moment there, as Pat was saying, when brain functioning slows down. Most people are taken by the slowing down. There is a critical moment when you must see this slowing down also as an object, bring the seen back to the seeing as you say, and stay in awareness.

Yes. Then the energy spent in objectifying is transferred to the subject, the seeing. The relaxed brain is an object. It has nothing to do with the "I am." When there's identification with the relaxed brain there's sleepiness.

Is the relaxed brain then something like a key? Because when the brain is relaxed it's clearer.

The relaxed brain is a perfect vehicle. It belongs to the mind and all that you see, that you touch, is mind. When you look around you, it is all mind. There is only mind.

The scientist says, "This object has independent reality." That is only the point of view of certain scientists. But the potentiality of the object is in your awareness. It is you who project it.

Would you say something about the desire for desirelessness that comes from the source?

I think that when we speak of desire, our fundamental desire is desirelessness. Because the moment a desired object is attained, you can see for yourself there is a moment which is completely timeless. The object is not present and you, as you, are not present. There is an absence of yourself and the so-called cause of the desirelessness. There is only the desireless, peaceful state. Only being. But after this non-state you say, "It is this or that which is the cause of this state. It is myself who has been in this state." But the moment you live it really, it is absolutely a non-dual experience.

When you live in reality is there any variety of experience?

When you live in reality there is no longer an experiencer. Any experience brings you immediately to the non-experience. It is immediately dissolved in your presence. It is immediately absorbed by presence. Like a magnet.

So does this background presence or awareness have any particular relationship to the body that . . .

The body appears in awareness. There is only awareness. There are projections in form and name, but you can qualify them also as only consciousness.

I think you should more and more become familiar with thought-free observation, with direct perception. Many residues from the past will come up from the many levels of the psychosomatic body.

I remember you once said when looking at something, that instead of having our eyes go out to grasp it, we should let the object come to us. Would that be the same when allowing the feeling and perceptions of the body to come to us?

Absolutely. The body is an object like any other. Instead of looking at the object, the object looks at you. This relaxes all your nervous system. All the optic nerves become relaxed and also the body.

When I have been just sitting quietly, it seems at times the thoughts come from far away and they just come into the welcoming and leave, but then there is a thought that almost feels like it is close to my throat in some way,

151

like a little thought says something like, "Come back to your breath," or "Remember the space," or whatever. It's harder to let that be. Should I treat this kind of thought with a different kind of attention?

You should allow all thought products to come and to go. Neither produce them nor repel them. Ignore them. Don't make any discrimination there.

I have a question about anger. I wondered, when I am around someone who is angry—either talking to me with angry feelings or angry directly at me—I often experience a sense of wanting to diffuse it or possibly move away in some way. I wonder if anger can actually be a toxicant on the body level or if I'm reacting?

When somebody is angry with you and you are identified with your body, you react; but when you are not identified with your body, it goes through you. The moment you react, you fuel the other.

But anger is not always a reaction. It could also be simply an action. When somebody doesn't act according to the truth, there may be an action which, from outside, looks like reaction, like anger; but it is not a reaction, not anger.

You have said that there are moments when there is simply seeing, when nobody sees and nothing is seen. Is this seeing still a brain function?

No, it is not a function. This seeing is consciousness. The organ which sees is an expression of awareness. When there is seeing, as you said, nobody sees and nothing is seen. There is only seeing. Can you localize this seeing? No.

Is seeing still an object that appears in the I-principle?

Absolutely. Because in this seeing there is no object-object. That you speak of a subject-object is memory. But when you see a flower, there is only seeing. When you say, "I see a flower," then it is a concept. When you say, "I saw the flower," it is a concept too. But you cannot see a flower and, at the same moment, think, "I see the flower and it is a flower which belongs to this or this species." When the quality and the characteristics come in, it is the mind which is evaluating, comparing and then there is subject-object relationship. In the moment of direct, pure observation, there is no subject-object relationship. When there is really pure seeing, direct seeing, take note how it acts on you. It is very interesting to feel how completely free you feel and how the energy of all the many levels of the psychosomatic body comes up.

Is this seeing itself an object of your awareness?

No. No. It is awareness.

Did you say that it was not an object, but that it was awareness itself?

Yes.

There are no objects in awareness?

Awareness is not an object. All that could become an object is in awareness, has its potentiality in awareness.

I mean, is awareness aware of the brain looking or is awareness itself looking at it?

The brain is a tool.

Is there any intermediary between the looking and awareness? Is the looking directly into awareness?

When there is looking, there is awareness looking. It is only awareness. But the moment your looking is intentional, or you look for a result, then your looking is relative. But when you walk in the forest or you walk in the mountain, your attention is completely free from all intention. You may name things, but that belongs to our language, to our culture. But the moment you qualify and interpret it, then it is the mind which comes and interferes and there is choice and there is selection. When there is selection and choice, there is misery and there is pain.

So awareness uses the brain as a tool?

Awareness doesn't "use," it is. It cannot ever be perceived because you are the perceiving. Like the eye can never see its seeing.

There may be moments when you walk in the mountains without naming or qualifying. You are just pure observation. Suddenly there is a bird and it is the bird which makes you aware that you are in silence. It is the object, bird, which makes you aware that there is silence. That is why in Chinese or Japanese paintings there is often much space in the picture so that the object points to the emptiness. Like the bird, who is calling, points to the emptiness, makes you aware of it.

Am I right, then, in assuming that the various senses are the vehicles of awareness in some way?

Yes.

Awareness manifests through the senses. There is also, however, this overall feeling that you are talking about, which seems, in some way, to cut across the senses or to incorporate all the senses. Then it seems to me there is a kind of ability to know that this is happening. Is that right? The example that you just gave a minute ago of being in the silence and the bird coming and reminding you that you are in the silence, is that the only way that we can know that we are in the silence—the movement from the object seen to the pure seeing, the awareness?

When you live knowingly in silence, of course, the object, the bird, doesn't reveal anything, because you are knowingly in the silence. But when you live unknowingly in the silence, then the bird may be the object which points to the silence.

Interesting. Because when I sat down I felt extraordinarily appreciative of the fact that you help us remember or stay in touch with the silence. My question was, what am I going to do next week or the week after when I don't see you; and, in a way, I guess the answer is what you just said. Objects—any object—can remind me.

Yes, if you look at it innocently. Contact first the space around the object. This space is your own space, make it your own and then from your own space go to the object. Go around. Go behind. Look, like a painter or a poet.

Does the experience of space change as you live more this timelessness?

Space is stillness. It is a symbol for silence. When you look at space, become perfectly attuned to it. Be in identity with it. Make it your own experience. There is no subject-object relationship. When there is subject-object relationship, you fix it in front of you. When the subject-object relationship is eliminated, you feel it somehow behind you. But this is only a geometrical representation, a pedagogical device. In reality it is neither behind nor in front, nor left nor right, because it is objectless. I remember Sri Atmananda Krishna Menon saying, "First you must find yourself behind and then later you will also find yourself in front, left and right and up and down." I think this feeling of being behind is akin to the movement we make when we want a good look at something. We take a few steps backwards to feel and see it more globally.

When we live more in this space, does the feeling of hereness, being here, dissolve?

When you attune yourself to the space, there is only space. It is a thought-free moment.

Is the same true of time?

In reality there is no time. Time begins only when the mind functions, when there is thinking. Time is created by thinking. The evolution of time needs space. And space evolution needs time. Time and space can never be separated. But the *real* that I am and that you are is timeless. When you live in the now, there is no time. In any case, past and future are memory. When you think of the past, it is a present thought. You label it 3,000 years ago or yesterday. But this is every time a present thought.

155

ON MEDITATION

As long as there is any residue of a meditator and something meditated on, then you make meditation an activity of the mind. Every activity is a contraction. Meditation is not an activity of any kind.

Feel yourself vertical, but don't try to *make* yourself vertical. When you feel that you are vertical you are in the timeless. All action is on the horizontal plane. Meditation is where time and timeless meet—in the heart.

Have the sensation of your whole body. Feel it in space. Go completely into the space that doesn't belong to time. Dissolve totally in this expansion.

Meditation is from moment to moment. The eyes see, the ears hear. The organs function. There is no interiorization, no concentration, no introversion, no withdrawing of the senses. Don't go into the old habits of withdrawal. Go in the directionless expansion, the spaceless space. This is not *nirvikalpa samadhi* (which is still in a very subtle subject-object relationship). It is not *savikalpa samadhi* (direct perception). It is *sahaja*. *Savikalpa* is perceiving and *nirvikalpa* is conceiving. *Sahaja* is the natural non-state where function takes place in beingness.

London, England

July 1989

An English college between semesters. A feeling of emptiness. The original fine Regency house overgrown with drab modern extensions and teaching blocks. We wandered around the lake, sat on the lawns and admired the roses in the sunken rose garden. We met, slept and ate in functional schoolrooms. We forgot the visiting TV film crew, the week-end seminar for computer scientists, the noise from the Heathrow flight path, and turned towards that silence in which all sights and sounds appear and disappear...

T HIS IS A NONCONVENTIONAL MEETING, a nonconventional talk, a thanking. So if there is anything that is not clear, please push me into the corner in order to make it clear!

First I would like to talk about what I mean by listening. Listening is not a function; it is not any activity; it is neither inside nor outside. It is timeless, and to come to this timeless listening you should only become aware when you are not listening; that is enough. When you see that you don't listen, come back to the seeing, bring the seen back to the seeing; then you are in timeless listening. When this listening is sustained it expands and comes to stillness. It is only when what you have understood on the intellectual level is completely dissolved in listening, when there is no more representation, that there is stillness. Everything to which you listen refers to the listening, has its homeground in listening, in stillness. In listening and stillness there is nobody who is still, and this stillness doesn't refer to any object; it is absolutely objectless; it is our real nature; it is our globality.

Have you any questions?

In that state of listening, that state of being, what is there to listen to?

When there is listening in its natural state, in its innocent state, this listening is being listening; it is not in a subject-object relationship.

You cannot localize it, you cannot represent it, you cannot feel it, you cannot think it because there is nobody to feel it and nobody to think it; there is nothing to feel and nothing to think.

Are you saying there is a difference between listening and hearing?

The listening of which we are speaking doesn't refer to the specific organ of our ear, it refers to our totality; it is total listening, total openness and receiving. Your real nature is only this listening, this receiving, free from any localization.

So I hear my voice, but I listen to you?

Yes. (laughter) When you listen to music, your ear plays a very small role; in listening to music you hear with your whole body.

Who is it who listens?

In global listening there is no place for an independent entity, there is nobody who listens; there is only listening. All your surroundings refer to this listening. There is listening occasionally to something, but when there is nothing to listen to, there is only listening, beingness. Your real nature is in a total state of "I don't know," of not-knowing. Real knowing is only in not-knowing. When you remain in knowing on the intellectual plane, there is still conflict; knowledge must completely dissolve in not-knowing, then in not-knowing you really know.

What is the difference between not-knowing and confusion?

As long as you refer your not-knowing to possible knowing, there is confusion. All possible knowing must completely dissolve in not-knowing. In knowledge, you remain in the mind; in not-knowing you feel your globality. It is only in not-knowing that there is joy. So you must understand very clearly that when you say, "I know," you really don't know. You have fixed the known as a thought only, as a representation. Really *being* knowing is when all representation has dissolved in not-knowing; only in this not-knowing is there knowing.

I didn't catch what you said—"Knowing on the intellectual plane is ..."?

On the intellectual plane, on the plane of the mind there is duality. When you say, "I know," your knowing refers to not-knowing, and when you say, "I don't know," it refers to eventual knowing. So you remain in duality. So to really know your real nature, you must come to the double not-knowing.

When I see that I am not listening, how can just seeing this help me to be in listening?

When you see that you don't listen, when not listening is seen, you are the seer. So the seeing that you don't listen, the object, is brought back to the seeing, the subject. Coming back to the seeing means coming back to consciousness, to openness. When you take note of something, you are out of the process. So bring the seen back to the seeing; bring what is heard back to the hearing.

What do you mean by "bring it back"?

When you see something, that which is seen is not outside of you, it has its potentiality in you. It is you who project it; it is an energy that you project in space and time. You feel this eccentric energy that you project, but you can also make it concentric. When you see something and you are fixed on the seen, then I would say, close your eyes, relax and let it come back to the seeing. When it comes back to the seeing there is nothing more seen, you are the seeing.

It is not a process of volition. When you see something you project it in space and time, as we said; it has its homeground in seeing. Let it come back to the seeing; it's not a process of volition.

So it's a process of letting-go?

Yes, of letting-go. It is a waiting without waiting; it is a waiting which is open.

Could you talk about the physiological state of the body, what is the actual physiological state when one is in listening? When the object comes back to the seeing, are we in deep relaxation?

The body must be completely free from all anticipation and expectation, free from any residue from the past. It must be completely relaxed. So, to come to an understanding, an experience of listening, we must first take our body as an object of observation. The moment we take our body as an object of observation, we will see that we know only certain fractions of our body and it may be very difficult to feel the whole body. In these fractions there are contractions, heaviness and reactions. So the moment our body becomes an object of innocent observation—and by innocent I mean that the observer is free from expectations and free from memory—then in this innocent observation there is no place for an "I", a "me," which created the reactions and heaviness. There is no longer an accomplice to keeping the contractions in the body, and they become free. Then we come to a global, empty feeling of our body. What we call unconditioned observation, innocent looking, has everything to do with a body which is free from any grasping or taking.

So when we really listen, we are free from all tension?

Yes, in this listening to the body all tension disappears and we come to the unconditioned body. You free yourself from all the residues of the past. In innocent observation there is accepting. You can never observe something when you don't accept it, so first there must be acceptance. In accepting your pain, your pain changes. It is only an object which can have pain, and you are not the object but the observer of it. I don't say there is no pain, but the pain is reduced to its bare, functional aspect. In psychological resistance you are an accomplice with the pain. It is only in accepting that the body takes itself in charge, because the origin of the body is health, the origin of the body is perfection.

Dr. Klein, could you say something more about everything we see being a projection?

Generally we think that an object exists outside ourselves, that it has an independent existence, but that is only a belief. It is not based on experience or fact. The so-called object outside of us needs consciousness to be perceived. Consciousness and its object are one, so you create, you project, the world from moment to moment. When the body first wakes up in the morning, at the same moment the world wakes up. You project the world; it is you who creates the world from moment to moment.

Do you mean that action creates the world as we see it, so that when I wake up in the morning and I see the room and what is in it, the room only exists when I wake up?

Firstly, when you wake up you don't see the room, you see only your memory. You see a corner of the ceiling and you say, "I'm in a room," but it is only memory which you are projecting and calling the room. Your seeing is only fractional. What you call your environment is certainly 80% memory.

When your listening is global, every moment is new, otherwise there is only repetition. As long as there is the reflex to take yourself for somebody you will see only fractions, and see your surroundings from a fractional point of view. It is this fractional seeing which creates a problem; otherwise there is no problem. So it is you who creates the problem.

Does that mean that all relationships will be something of a problem?

Absolutely! (laughter) Because real relationship is non-relationship. By non-relationship I mean free from being someone. When you take yourself for somebody you can only see a somebody. But when you live in the absence of the ego, you will only see the absence of the person in the so-called other. In this non-relationship is real relationship; otherwise there is only relationship from object to object, from person to person, and that is the cause of conflict. When you take yourself for a person you live in insecurity, since it takes effort to maintain the person, because the person cannot exist except in situations and is constantly in defense against the absence of situations. Enormous energy is wasted in creating situations, that is, a false continuity.

How do we let go of the person?

163

See that you take yourself for a somebody.

Seeing is very easy, but to let go is very difficult . . .

Seeing is not making a mental note, it means you see with more than your mind, how the seeing acts on you. You must give the seeing time. Don't rush on after taking note, but abide a while until you see how the seeing has affected you. When you see that for forty-two years you have been creating a person and that every-thing around you is seen from the point of view of this forty-two-year-old person, there is an impact. Take note of the impact. It is tremendous. In really feeling it is transformation; it is only this kind of seeing that has the power to transform. Otherwise there is only changing, and changing is not transmutation. Really seeing some-thing is transmutation; it is a kind of reorchestration of all your energy. Then you will one day be free from the person, and in this, your absence, there is only joy.

So if you don't actually feel something in your body, that means that you haven't seen it?

Precisely.

It is clear to me that, until now, seeing was just an idea, but the way you know that you have seen is when there is this perceiving in the body itself . . .

Yes, it must be perceived. The perceived is felt, it is not a concept.

When the insights remain intellectual, and you keep thinking, "I see it, I feel it," but you don't have this manifestation on the global level of the body, how do you bring the insight to the global level? How do you really feel something if you have had many insights, but they have remained more or less in the mind?

I would say, you must wait, wait until the known is completely dissolved in not-knowing. If, in order to understand an object, you look at another object, the knowledge remains in the realm of the already known. But when you ask the question, "Who am I? What is my real nature?" already all representation must be completely dissolved in being.

So you can say to yourself, "I've had an insight but it has not changed my life, it is only intellectual," and then you must go back to this bodily perception, the letting-go and relaxation?

Yes, when you have a clear global representation it acts on you, it acts on your whole body.

Like when suddenly one becomes aware of a tension and the tension disappears?

Of course, if you go to a psychoanalyst, he would say to you that this rising up of the shoulder is a psychological reaction. But that is only an explanation. To really understand the tension, you must feel your shoulder; your shoulder must be feeling. You listen to the feeling and then you will see that your shoulder drops down and further down until it finds its real position. You will also see that when the shoulder is completely down you are free from anxiety. So there is no explanation needed of why the shoulder goes up. You need only feel when the shoulder goes up, and it will automatically go down. This is an organic experience. Once you experience the right position, you will have an organic memory of it and immediately you will feel the difference when your shoulder is completely down and when it is up. From the moment that you see that every day you take yourself for somebody, that you identify yourself with your intelligence, capacities, talents and personality, and that you face the world and your surroundings from the point of view of this personality—when you *really* see what nonsense it is to take yourself for somebody that you are not really—then it will go away, you may be sure. One day you will be free from the person, suddenly free; that is a sudden enlightenment, to be free from the person. But when this happens, take note of it without justification, interpretation. When the mind comes in you can never come to transformation; it is consciousness which sees it, not the mind which sees it. It is very interesting and a tremendous shock when you see for one moment that you have taken yourself for Mr. Smith for forty-two years! That your personality is a complete fabrication, hollow, a shadow! It is a tremendous shock!

After that, then what, Dr. Klein?

After that you will sometimes taste yourself in your absence. You will really feel your real presence in this absence . . .

You have spoken of letting go of the shoulder as an example, and one sees similar activities taking place when letting go of the mind. One reaches a point where one has let go a lot, but then there is a tremendous fear to let go that last bit. There is still the desire to know, and the desire to know stops you letting go. Could you say something about that?

You can never separate the mind from the body, the body from the mind. The fear and anxiety that are felt at certain moments, you will feel first in your body-mind; but when you feel it you habitually transpose it onto the conceptual level and say, "I am in a state of fear." But when you say this, it is memory, a concept of fear; it is out of touch with the actual sensation. So free yourself from the concept fear and face only the perception. But face the perception unconditioned, free from all wishful thinking.

So "unconditioned" seems to be the operative word? When there is a continual desire for that extra bit, that desire causes the looking to be conditioned?

Yes. Try to find the desireless state in yourself. Look as a scientist looks, without interpretation, comparison, justification and so on. Come back every time to this pure perception. We know very little about pure perception because we immediately make it psychological, we make it a conception. When I speak of seeing it, that means seeing without interpretation, only facing the perception.

So it is without choice?

Yes, choiceless, without selection.

I mean, in my case, who chose to come here instead of going to the cinema?

I am not so sure! (laughter)

Neither am I!

I would like you to look a little more deeply at the motive which brings you here. When you look at the motive which brings you here, perhaps you can economize on your petrol consumption! You can face the problem immediately, in your sitting room. Maybe it is a lack of joy, a lack of peace, a lack of happiness. If it is lack of peace, perhaps you can face, in the moment itself, the sensation which makes you nervous. Face the perception in this moment, face the absence of peace and happiness, and you will find yourself not in the object, the lack or the nervosity, but in the seeing itself. You are the ultimate subject, the subject of all objects. Thousands and thousands of objects exist and change, but you are the only ultimate subject which can never become an object—so, be it; there is your freedom. When you really see it, it will strike you as evident that there is nothing to attain, nothing to achieve. If somebody says that you can learn something or achieve insight through a technique or a system, go away from them. All that takes you away from real seeing. There is nothing to attain, because you are it. In trying to attain it you go away from it because it is your nearest. Before the body wakes up in the morning, you are. It is enough that you know that the waking state, dreaming state and sleeping state are *in* you. What is behind all states is your real nature, your real face; it is the same face that you had before you were born, and it is the same face that remains after your physical death. But what is important is that you integrate it knowingly.

I don't know that moment you speak of before the mind wakes up. I feel that I go from unconscious deep sleep or dreams, to the "normal" waking state.

There are moments when the body is not completely a body, and the world is not completely a world, so remain in this perfume of deep sleep, be completely attuned to it. Don't force your body-

167

mind to work or wake up, don't force the world to be a world. You will see, when you really do this, that the whole day has this feeling of the background.

So it's a matter of staying with that feeling before the body-mind wakes up?

Yes, you cannot do it by will, but the moment you feel it, be completely attuned to the feeling, be one with the feeling; you can never keep it, it keeps you.

Dr. Klein, how can daily activities get done if there is no personality and no ego?

In your absence you will feel your real presence. All that appears in your life is like that which appears on a stage, but you don't identify yourself with the person on the stage, you simply remain in the hall and be the witness. Real joy is when you are the witness to all that appears and disappears. Then your relationships will change completely, because there is no personality with which you are identified. The personality is a very good, useful tool, but you don't identify yourself with the personality. You act spontaneously and this acting is not reacting, it is really appropriate to every moment. Spontaneous acting means there is no actor, there is no doer, there is only action. There is no entity in the cosmos, there is only functioning. And functioning without the interference of the personality belongs to the new age.

What did you mean when you said, "There is no entity in the cosmos"? Surely there is some universal being that uses us as a kind of tool, and we are being used in a very natural way by that which is other than us? There is no form, but there is something other than us which is operating the whole show? Or don't you believe in God?

There is not an operator, there is only operation. There is not an operator. This question is completely different when you feel your-self in your real nature, but the moment you feel yourself an isolated individual, you take yourself for something unique and separate.

Would you say that the problem with human beings is that we think too much, and place too much importance on those thoughts, and we then see the world according to our thoughts instead of seeing the world as it is—and therefore our thoughts, which are the product of memory, our science, experience and knowledge, are the things which create every conflict that mankind has experienced?

It brings us to the question: What is thought? What is thinking? What is the moment when you start to think? When you go deeper you will see that your thinking starts from thinking. This thinking is only reaction, nothing else. But you also know another way of thinking; this thinking starts from silence. Thinking which starts from thinking keeps you in a vicious circle, it is only repetition. Thinking which starts from silence is creative thinking, creative living and doing and feeling. Real thinking is going away from thinking, so free yourself from thinking!

Can you explain what you mean when you say, "Thinking starts from thinking"?

Thinking starts from thinking only when there is an "I," when there is a "me," otherwise there is only spontaneous thinking. Spontaneous thinking starts from non-thinking. When I say, "Free yourself from thinking," that means free yourself from thinking which only has its roots in the "I" concept, the "I," the "me," memory. The "I," the "me," is psychological memory, past, future, but when you are free from the "I" you are only in the now.

When there is an absence of the psychological entity is that when the divine play happens?

It is only in the absence of yourself that there is divine play. All that is expressed is an expression of life; it is in space and time. Generally we take the expressions of life to be life itself. Being life is this listening of which we are speaking, being listening, being still; there

169

is no entity to be still, there is only stillness and there is love. When you speak of a concept of God, where is God? It is nowhere; it is only here when you are not.

When you look at a tree, the tree is perceived through your five senses; it is seen, smelt, heard and so on. If the perceived is very attractive you may remain for a long time in pure perceiving where there is not a perceiver. But we generally escape from the perception by making it immediately a conception. We judge it, compare it; we use it—mainly we use it. All interpretation is memory and it refers to the already known, but you know situations when you simply observe from point to point without interpretation until there is a global impression without interpretation. It is taking note, only seeing facts until, at a certain moment, there is an instantaneous upcoming of the whole picture. This understanding is not the result of the mind; it comes from the situation itself. It is only by seeing the situation as a whole that you are brought to action which is not reaction, but acting according to the situation.

You spoke of the observer, but I find the observer is just another thought.

Absolutely. The controller is also a thought.

So at that moment it seems to me that there is no perception, it is total conception?

There must be only perception where you are completely aware, clear-minded, and you take note of the situation.

Who takes note?

Consciousness.

So how do I eliminate this observer? Because I have been practising it for many years. The mind knows it is an illusion, but the reflex is still there to make the observer someone. I still believe I am the observer!

You know the wishes and ideas of the observer, but this observer is thought, seen by a witness. The observer which can be known belongs to the cage of the mind. You try to get out of this cage because you feel uncomfortable, not at peace, insecure. But when you see that the observer belongs to the cage, then what happens? You stop.

Never try to know the witness. The witness is not a function. The witness cannot be perceived. Just take it for granted from me, that you are, in any case, the witness.

I think my problem is that I don't seem to stop the cycle of thoughts. I think the observer is a thought, but that is another thought; then that's a concept as well.

The moment that you see it, let go of the object, the idea of the observer or the feeling of being an observer, and feel yourself in the seeing. Now I would say, feel yourself behind yourself! There is a moment when you feel yourself behind yourself. In a certain way it feels at first like a localization behind, at the base of the skull.

I see that, but I conceptualize it again . . .

You must not; you must feel it as a global feeling.

What happens when the thought immediately comes up, "Now I am behind"?

All thoughts are in the forehead so you cannot be behind and at the same time think, "I am behind." In feeling oneself behind, you feel only a tremendous energy. This energy is not the directed power to strike the brain and form a concept. It remains only energy. It doesn't come to any formulation of "I am this or that."

So there is an awareness of the energy in globality, but there's no thought?

Absolutely. Completely thought-free.

But there is a desire to grab that energy, to do something with that energy, to bring it to a function . . .

You are still master of this energy, it is still orchestrated in a certain way by you. You are aware that it is not coming to conceptualization. It is important for you, at this moment, to feel yourself behind yourself. This feeling behind yourself can be compared to the kind of tactile sensation you have when you sit there and let all the tactile sensation behind your body come up as you contact the wall behind you. You are certainly able to do this—not as an idea but as a feeling, a sensation. This tactile sensation is more or less at the surface, but the feeling of being behind, that I am speaking of, is very strong. For one second there may still be some duality—that there is a feeler and something felt—but the feeler and what is felt disappear too, and there is only being the feeling.

So at that moment one experiences what you mean by "consciousness is one with its object"?

Yes, absolutely.

There is a quotation from the Bible which says, "The birds have their nests, the foxes their holes, but the Son of Man has nowhere to lay His head." It just seems that we would love to have somewhere to lay our heads. Could you say something about that?

We can see that we are completely identified with the personality. We take ourselves for our personality, and this taking ourselves for our personality immediately causes insecurity, because the personality can only exist in a continual situation. That is why we constantly create situations from the past, and projections into the future. We prefer a bad situation to none at all. So we must see how, in daily life, we are constantly creating situations for the survival of personality. We live constantly in end-gaining. This is the first insight we must have. It is useless to pursue truth and enlightenment. You can only see what is not truth, what is not clarity. You cannot see truth with the mind because you are truth. You can never see the light because you are it. Just as the eye cannot see its own seeing.

You may not have had the exact answer to your question, but when you have understood what I have said, you will see it is the answer to your question. The personality belongs to knowledge. It is a very important tool in our daily life, but to identify yourself with it you will see is nonsense.

What is the function of obedience in letting go of the personality?

I need to ask you for clarification.

What is the role of surrender in being faced with constant choice, "Thy will be done"?

You *are* choiceless. In choicelessness you are free from the personality. The personality comes and goes like any tool. As long as you identify yourself with your personality there is intention, there is selection, there is choice and choosing whether to choose. But you know moments in daily life when there is completely choiceless living, without selection, free from memory. You take these moments as an absence of something, but in this absence of activity there is really presence. You superimpose an absence of activity where there is presence.

Usually people who are on this search will go to India, or to some quiet place. Is it really possible for those of us living in the very busy western world to come to this experience?

But the problem in London, in Delhi, in Berlin and in Paris is always the same problem! The problem may be formulated and addressed in another way but it is the same problem.

You don't need the quietness of a retreat?

Yes, London is a quiet place! (laughter) The problem is nowhere except the moment itself, so face the problem immediately there where it is.

Thank you!

WHEN YOU SAY, "I UNDERSTAND," in reality you haven't understood, because the understanding has been localized in a concept in your brain. Real understanding is when the concept and the percept have completely vanished in silence, in your totality, in your globality, in your wholeness. You can never force the understanding, you cannot try to understand; you can only live with your question. Living with your question means to have a silent relationship with your question. When you have that silent relationship, the question unfolds, and vanishes in the living answer. What you are fundamentally can never become an object, something perceived. But everything you are looking for can only be an object. However, you know you are the ultimate subject, the knower, the subject of all objects. So looking for an answer in a world of objects is a complete waste of time. When this really hits you, what happens? There is a stop and automatically, spontaneously, the subject refers to itself; that is your wholeness, your globality. The energy which was projected returns to you.

This is only to say, "Hello" to you! (laughter) Are there any questions?

Should one address the question to oneself and see what comes up—is that what you are saying?

Yes, but you must first know how to live with your question; you must not try and force the answer. If you try to force the answer you project memory, you project the already known. So your question must rest in silence. Because when you become more and more ripe, you will see that the answer is the question, the looker is what is looked for.

So the question is in a sense the answer then?

Yes. But you must be ripe for the answer, and when you become ripe for the answer then you have the right behavior in living with the question. Because the answer doesn't go through the mind, the answer is instantaneous. When you live with your question in this silence there is already a kind of fore-feeling of the answer, of the living answer.

How does one actually stop taking oneself for an object and just realize that one is?

You cannot take yourself for an object because an object always needs a subject. The object changes but the subject never changes. The projected object can be dressed in various ways, but it always belongs to the already known. When you say you have found something new, or that science has found something new, it is never new, it is the old, colored in different ways. But the subject never changes.

So one realizes that the answer doesn't lie in looking for objects, and then you naturally give up, and that is the way?

Yes, you give up looking for an object, because you know you can never be an object.

You have talked about "taking note." Could you say a bit more about taking note?

In taking note there is no psychological interference; you look at facts as they are, without interpretation or justification. The facts then belong to your completeness, to your totality. The solution is always in the facts, in the situation itself. The person can never find the solution; it may find a temporary solution, but this solution always comes to a conflict in the end. It is only when you are open to all the facts that you come to right understanding and right action. When you see your surroundings from the point of view of the ego, of the person, from a fraction, you can only see fractions. Real understanding comes when you see the situation in its totality from the ultimate.

You said we must be ripe to ask a question, but it seems that this ripeness would render a question obsolete.

When you live in your totality, in your completeness, there is no question, but where there is a lack of peace or joy in you, that brings you to the question. But it needs a certain maturity to come to the question and to really formulate the question.

Is the question different for everybody, or is there one ultimate question?

There are many questions, but these many questions bring you to the one question, and the only one question is: "Who am I? What is life?" All other questions turn around and point to this ultimate question.

Have you a personality?

I have an arm to hold something, I have a leg to walk with, and I have a personality to function in the same way. It is a tool, a useful tool. But what I am is nothing objective; that means you can never see me, never hear me, never touch me.

But I can see you, and I can hear you—just about!

A very good way to see me is to close your eyes!

Dr. Klein, where does maturity come from?

Maturity comes from inquiring, inquiring about your life, your motives, your surroundings, your relationships. Inquiring means questioning, seeing facts and questioning the facts, without forcing an answer, without forcing a solution, only taking note. Because you will eventually see that your real nature is openness: you cannot assert it, you can never fix it; it is openness, it is constant interrogation.

Why is it that some people have certain gifts they want to express?

I would say that the deep feeling of joy and peace brings you to express it, to share it, and certain people have the gift to express it in painting, sculpture or poetry, in theatre, in music and so on. This talent is a tool for offering, for thanking—there is nobody who thanks—it is simply the deep desire to give thanks that you are, that you are allowed to be.

It seems to me that life is very much like a tea party for a child, who comes in and sits down and there are all these jellies and cakes and lovely toys to play with, like his mind and body, and all these other wonderful things that we have to play with . . . and I'm wondering if this sense of "I" is not also part of creation just like a toy. How can one know?

The body-mind is given to you to express what you feel very deeply. It gives you the possibility to become what you are fundamentally, that's all; the first birth gives you the opportunity to be really born.

You said the ultimate question is: Why are we here? What conclusion have you formed for why you are here?

I have not formed any conclusion; it is only a big pleasure to be with you!

I don't mean here this evening! Why do you exist, Dr. Klein?

I am what I am, and this has nothing to do with existence.

But you are talking about two different "I's," aren't you? There is Dr. Klein and there is the ultimate "I," and they don't have any connection?

To ask, "What is life?" is a very serious question, a very deep question; it requires earnestness. You will see that what you call life are the expressions of life, the extensions of life, but not life itself. So every question that you formulate must directly refer to its source, which is your quietness. When your question is related to your quietness, it is sacred, and then it comes to the living answer. All that exists appears in tranquility and dissolves in silence and tranquility. So, when we speak of relationship it is only in this quietness that there is relationship, because relationship refers only to this quietness, this silence. Relationship from object to object, personality to personality, doesn't refer to quietness. This so-called relationship is only looking for security, for psychological survival. Real relationship, real love, is in this quietness, in this silence.

When we feel love and joy and gratitude, who is feeling, and where do these feelings come from?

In these feelings there is not a feeler, there is only feeling.

They seem to come when we are absent, as you said, but what are these great qualities, and where do they reside?

When we are completely absent, then we are totally present! It is only in our absence that there is totality, that there is presence. But joy, love, peace, can never be put in the frame of the mind, because the mind can never really understand joy, peace and love. The mind may have an echo of it, but love, peace and joy are completely non-dual; they are not in subject-object relationship.

I notice that when I want to sit quietly, I escape immediately to something else, so I wonder whether asking questions is another escape, and whether there is a better way?

There may also be an opportunity to ask a question. By opportunity I mean you are ready to receive the answer. But very often the answer is not formulated; so, rather than try to formulate the answer in those moments, live only with the essence of the answer, the essence of the formulation. Because when you try to formulate the essence it is already a reduced answer. The living answer precedes the formulation. So really live with the essence.

You said the ultimate question is: Who am I? To me that prompts the question: Is there such a thing as a creator? On your path have you found a creator?

When you ask yourself, "What is life? Who am I?" what happens in this moment? You are free from any representation, you live in a state of total "I don't know;" you live in a complete not-knowing where there is no reference to anything, because you have understood that you can never find yourself in an object, that you are not the object, that you are the ultimate subject. So you live completely in not-knowing.

Are you saying that you don't know anything about anything?

Exactly! You are totally present, but only because you are totally absent; you are in a state of waiting without waiting for anything.

But don't you think that to function in the world one has to form certain conclusions about what the world is for, and how you should act in the world?

That question can only come afterwards, when you know what you are. You understand the world only when you know what you are, then you will see that the world belongs to you; you are the world. Let us not fall into the trap of keeping the understanding in the mind; let the understanding dissolve in your totality. Otherwise, if the question remains in your mind it will turn into yet a new question and so on and so on. To allow the understanding to flow in the body takes time, so don't immediately ask another question.

Dr. Klein, what is wisdom?

Wisdom belongs to knowledge, it belongs to being the knowing; that is wisdom.

You talked about ripeness earlier. How can we ripen?

Ripening comes through inquiring, inquiring into your life, your feelings, your thinking, your surroundings, your relationship with your husband, with your children, and so on. Inquiring means that you are completely open. When you inquire, when you question, never force an answer, because the right attitude in asking a question is the answer. So when you inquire into your life the attitude must be: I am open to not-knowing, and from this opening to not-knowing comes the answer. The answer is on a completely different plane from the question.

What is functional acceptance, which you have often talked about?

Functional acceptance is seeing facts. The moment you try to interpret them, justify or manipulate them, you are not really accepting them. When you see facts from your globality, there is welcoming without choice. When you look from the ego, there is psychological acceptance, which is not acceptance. In real acceptance there is no personal manipulation.

When we do the yoga, you say, "Don't lose yourself". . .?

I mean not to identify yourself with what you are doing.

But if one has an awareness all the time of not identifying, then one is in duality, one is observing and something is observed . . .

When you are lost in what you are doing, you are in bondage; but when you are alert, then the object, what you are doing, is in your awareness, and you are not in the object. Then immediately you will feel space between your observation and the observed. By space, I mean silence or quietness.

I am not quite clear on the difference in feeling between "being lost in the object" and "consciousness and its object are one."

When you are lost in the object, it is a kind of daydreaming. There is a moment when you "wake up" and say, "I was absent." Being lost in the object is a temporary state. But when consciousness and its object are one, there is no change. Consciousness remains, and the object is lost in consciousness. There is no thought, "I am conscious," because there is nothing else you could be! You simply *are*.

When you say, "You are the living answer to a question," does this approach hold true for every little question in daily life?

The ultimate answer is the answer for all the questions.

So the situation unfolds in all its details, and the details look after each other, because it is all just happening in awareness?

You must transpose the formulation in your own way. This gives you the security that you have really understood. The transposition is very important. When you can transpose the fact onto another level, it shows you have really understood.

When you say, "See the facts," how can I know what the facts are, because when I look, there is an immediate interpretation, which is not the facts.

See your immediate reflex to interpret, and that you can only interpret through the already known. That is enough. But life is not repetition, the facts of life are new every time.

So there is nothing to refer to at all when I really see the facts?

It is the "I," the "me," the person, who tries to interpret, because the person can only exist in situations where it finds security. So see when the reflex to interpret comes up; then you will remain in direct perception.

So all my reactions are also part of the fact?

Yes, absolutely. And ask, "Who reacts?"

And any desire to stop that reaction is part of the reaction?

See the moment you react; make the reaction a perception. You perceive it, so face the perception. The moment you face the perception, the perception frees itself, and then you look again at the facts.

(long pause)

Be more and more acquainted in daily life with not formulating. When you walk in the forest and don't interpret, you remain in pure perception where there is no perceiver and nothing perceived.

When you speak of maturity, who is it who matures?

Maturity takes time, but it is an instantaneous revelation for you the moment you see that you take yourself for an entity. To really see what you are not, comes from maturity. It is maturity which brings you to the threshold of the "I am."

I still don't quite understand what you mean by maturity?

Maturity is seeing things clearly, seeing things in relation to this truth, to what you are. Maturity is when you see that things belong to your globality. Maturity brings you to the fore-feeling of what you are, it brings you, as I said, to the threshold of the "I am." And maturity only comes when you know the art of inquiring, questioning a situation without looking for an answer. Because the moment you question the situation without looking for the answer, the situation unfolds. The situation is much more than you know from your memory. But when you inquire, the situation—the expressions of life—unfolds. In this questioning you are completely open; you can only ask the question in openness, otherwise it is not a question. When an object asks the question there is never an answer; the answer is only fractional. And this answer then brings you again to a new conflict. But when this openness asks the question, this openness refers to itself. So, be open to the openness. It is a total global feeling, a feeling of the "I am." When you ask the question in this way, see what happens in your psychosomatic body. Your whole system is completely expanded, open, and in this openness there is love—only then is there love. The "I" is nothing other than a contraction.

So what is important is to discover oneself in not-knowing. In not-knowing you will feel yourself in complete vastness, expansion, where there is no isolation. I would say there is a constant thanking. There is nobody who thanks, but it is a pleasure to thank, because all minerals, vegetables, animals have helped you to be here. Our surroundings—the moon, the sun, the stars—have all helped you to become a human being. So, in your openness there is constant thanking.

So there is nobody who thanks, but you give thanks for being . . .?

It's only an inner urge to thank, to give thanks that you are.

Why is there an urge to thank?

I think as long as you are a human being there is thanking, gratitude for being, not for being human, but for being what you fundamentally *are*. Thanking for the sake of thanking.

If you feel ill and a virus attacks you, would you feel thankful then?

Absolutely! Because there is nothing accidental in this life.

But would we have bothered about medicine and science if we had given thanks for everything?

Be thankful for whatever appears to you, don't react, only admire. What appears is only a pointer, it points to something and you must accept it. In this acceptance there is understanding. It is only an object which suffers, but you are not an object; you are the ultimate subject, you are the ultimate perceiver. Inquire: Who is the perceiver? You will never find it, because you are it—so, be it!

*W*HEN A PERSON DEEPLY PERCEIVES *that the observer, the experiencer, the ego, is basically an illusion, does it cease to exist by just watching and listening?*

The mind must know what is beyond its capacity, then the mind is open to a new dimension. As long as there is an "I," the mind is never open, it is split; there is choice and selection. The mind can never know what is beyond the mind, but the mind can be open. What we call a personality, an "I," is an accumulation of knowledge, secondhand information, education and so on. It has no more value than identifying yourself with your memory.

Can you define the meaning of mind?

The mind is a function.

If mind is a function, then what is behind the function?

We are behind the function, we are the light behind every perception and conception. Non-intentional attention is your real nature; this attention is open.

I have very tantalizing glimpses of what you are saying, yet there always seems to be another cause, another step needed. I get the impression that it's a never-ending process.

Steps exist only in the mind. What is important is that you come to the deep conviction that you are the ultimate subject, the ultimate subject of all concepts, all percepts, of all objects. Because all that you can achieve, all that you can obtain, is in the realm of the mind. When you have this conviction, there is a stop. You must discover your whole being in this moment of the stop. It is not only an intellectual understanding; your whole being is in openness, is attending, but not attending to anything, is waiting without waiting. You can discover yourself only in your absence.

There are lots of thoughts and feelings and emotions that over the years one suppresses. You don't actually get a chance to see them but one has to see them in order to know that you are not them. But how can one actually see them when one is habitually suppressing them?

Face the body, senses and mind. Inquire, explore, remembering that you can only explore and inquire with a completely open mind, free from all expectation, anticipation, and end-gaining. The moment the observation is more free from anticipation and expectation, you get a glimpse of this reality. There is a flow of energy, since the energy you have put on the observed comes back to the observer. Then you are open to the openness. It is a very still listening, I would say, a still listening to the perception, not to the conception, only to the perception. You asked what happens in the body. The body and all its reactions and residues are perceived. The body is an expression of listening, an expression of silence, an expression of consciousness; it has its homeground, its potentiality in consciousness, in listening. In a certain way it is a pointer, it brings you back to your real nature. It is really a way of discovering this very deep love.

What is the value in doing the exercises and postures?

It takes time to come to the right posture because the postures are archetypes. By archetype I mean here a certain posture which includes all the positions. In doing the one, you face the many. The approach to the body is to reorchestrate the dispersed energy, nothing else. It brings you to a state of fitness and clearness, transparency, where you are available for ultimate understanding. As the mind and body are interdependent, the readiness and lightness of the body play a role in understanding. In exploring the body you become more and more able to know the body. In exploring you are completely aware of the body, and it is only in this awareness that the body comes to this reorchestration of the dispersed energy. But, of course, you must undertake this exploration knowing that you are not the body.

But if the insight into our real nature has nothing to do with the mind or body, what difference does it make what our bodies do?

Of course, what we are fundamentally has nothing to do with the body. One can never come to being the understanding through the body. But we are trapped in our mind and body and we must become free of this entrapment so that understanding can take place in us. It is commonly understood that the body is a hindrance to awakening, but to disregard the body because of this superficial observation is a mistake. One must discover what is the nature of this hindrance; we must understand it. Because truth can never be attained, only welcomed, we must bring our body-mind to the welcoming state.

I notice as I pass through the world that I tend to make comments, to name things; if I go through a wood I name all the trees and it seems that the mind must grapple with whatever is in front of it. I see this as unhelpful, but to meet it head on and try and stop it, is that helpful? Or is there another way of meeting the creation and the tendency to comment on it, and turning this to some sort of use in one's development?

When you see an object and name it, it belongs to your culture, your education. Even if you were living on an island and you saw certain objects in the sky or heard a certain noise, you would still refer it to something that you know. This is normal and I don't see any problem in naming it. But when you go further and interpret, judge, qualify it, in this moment you are isolated from the object, because you are in the mind with your opinions, in memory, and not one with the perception. So, it may be advisable for you to remain from time to time in pure observation, where there is no observer or something observed. When we go immediately from the percept to the concept, we introduce psychological intervention between ourselves as the observer and what we observe.

So the moment we conceptualize, we begin to lose touch with reality, is that what you are saying?

Yes, you are isolated and lose the actuality, I would say. There is no repetition in life; it is we who superimpose repetition on it.

So what does one do about it, just watch the mind playing games, or what?

You will become aware when your surroundings refer to yourself as being somebody. You will see that if it's convenient and secure for you, then you identify yourself with it. But if it represents insecurity then you push it into the unconscious, you push it away and escape. Generally we function in this way. So I would say: Be interested in how you function in daily life, explore without any criticism or justification. Simply take note; that is enough. The moment you take note that you always see your surroundings from the point of view of your personality, that this is a fact, then there is a stop. See how this insight acts on you. That is important. You see it, there is a stop, and you see your reaction. Your whole psychosomatic nature is included.

Then it's more helpful to observe the personality than to try and abolish it?

Absolutely! But this kind of observation has nothing to do with concentration, it is simply being aware of it.

You said when certain things make you feel insecure you push them away. So what happens, do they actually go away and not trouble you?

You can never push them away. Apparently you push them away, but you cannot push them away.

So where do they go?

There remains a certain residue in you.

When I try to meditate without intention, it seems to me very like daydreaming and my mind just seems to wander and get stuck in very concrete things in today, yesterday, tomorrow and in things like that. So I wonder if you have any guidance on how to prevent this getting lost in objects?

I think when you first go to meditation you must come to the conclusion that there is not a meditator. Because the meditator is a concept, it belongs to the mind and there is nothing to meditate on. So, with this conclusion—that there is not a meditator and nothing to meditate on—meditation immediately stops. Then there is only meditation! That is one thing. The second is, before you have a glimpse of what we understand by meditation—that is, what meditation is from moment to moment—you will discover moments in daily life when there is nothing to do, nothing to obtain, nothing to think, moments of complete emptiness of any activity. You know these moments, but as you know yourself only in connection with situations, you take these moments for an absence of activity. But the mind should know that these moments are the reality, are the background of all perceptions. When you have a glimpse from time to time of those moments, you may be invited to sit down and try—waiting in a certain way—for this glimpse again. That is the second proposition, and the third is that you simply sit down and free yourself from all concepts, and you can free yourself from all concepts the moment you direct your attention to the perception, to what is perceived. And then you look at your body, you listen to your body. When you listen to your body you may discover many things, but your listening will become more and more silent listening, free from achieving. So, when the body has, to a certain extent, given you its secret, you will feel yourself in this listening; you will listen to the listening and there is a change in the listening because you no longer emphasize the listened-to, but you listen to the listening itself. Listening becomes

189

its own perceiving without a perceiver, and this is meditation. So you have three ways to approach it. Do it also in the evening before going to sleep: the rent is paid, you are not hungry, everything is finished and you are free from all actions, then there is a moment when you can feel this freedom. The evening before you go to sleep is really a very good moment, because then it is easy to give up. In this way you learn how to give up and to be completely naked, so that only the "I am" remains. And then your waking up in the morning is different; you may have a glimpse of awakening before the body wakes up. One day there will be a moment when the body goes away forever, but the "I am" never goes away; the "I am" is. When you have really discovered the "I am," the problem of death doesn't come up any more; it doesn't even come to your mind.

Dr. Klein, you used the word "invitation" in our daily lives, and I want to know the nature of the person or the quality of the inviter.

Your real nature is waiting for it, so the invitation comes from your real nature.

There is a difference, though, between a pause in activity when there is nothing that needs to be done and one sits down to take advantage of it, but can the invitation come when one is very busy?

When you have once had a glimpse of what you are fundamentally, the invitation is stronger than all activities.

When you ask the question deeply, it brings you the answer, because the question is the answer. The discovery has nothing to do with time. According to your watch two minutes may pass, but the moment itself is timeless. What is important is that all your activities be at rest in this silence; then you are not psychologically involved in the function. It is important that you do not have the idea that you are a functioner, a doer, or a thinker. There is thinking, there is functioning, but there is no entity who functions. So you are completely free from all psychological involvement.

So it is doing without choice?

Yes, because there is no entity to choose.

These days there are many couples who don't stay together, so how can one find the right partner without choosing? (laughter)

In a certain way, seen from very high, when you are open, without preconceived ideas, the right partner comes to you, because there is no accident. But practically speaking (laughter) when you like poetry, literature, music, you will move in these circles where people love things that are beautiful. It is very important that you move in areas where there is beauty, for beauty is an expression of the highest non-state. You may not find beauty in bars or out on the street, but you will find it in a certain *milieu*! But I'm sure if you have the feeling to be a lovely human being, you will also find a lovely human being.

But is it right to expect another lovely human being to stay with you particularly? Because then one may say: Now you are mine and you have got to stay with me!

It is only beauty and love which keep the couple together. When there is not this beauty and love, it is only a relationship from object to object—female, male—and there comes a moment when the female is exhausted and the male is exhausted, and there is separation. But when you live in beauty and love there is constant transformation.

But when one lives in beauty and love, surely one wouldn't care whether a person stays with you or not? Is it only in an untrue relationship that you would expect the partner to stay with you?

In a relationship of object to object there is only demanding. Apparent giving is also demanding, because the giving is with a view to getting; but when there is love there is a non-relationship, and then there is only giving. When there is a relationship of object to object, sooner or later one is exhausted, because of this apparent giving and taking, and it comes to an end.

Sometimes there comes an insight that is pure and fresh, but then thought comes in and it is lost . . .

When you really see the facts around you, there is an insight which you must follow and keep warm. Then action comes spontaneously. Keep it for your own; it must be realized in space and time. It takes time, but you must keep it warm. When you don't keep it warm, then during the realization in space and time, you will lose it.

How do we keep it warm?

You look at it, you stay true to the feeling of it. When it goes through the discriminating mind, you begin a wheeling and dealing process. Don't bargain with your insight!

But that freshness, can it be lost forever?

I don't think so, but go back to the first incidence. You must not question it. For the realization of this insight, you must of course know your capital—intellectual, psychological, vital—and then your intelligence can function clearly.

From what you are saying it seems that this insight is so important that it is necessary before any action takes place?

It depends on what you have understood by insight.

An opening to a situation with the heart, with a knowledge of what it is and what is to come.

Yes. When there is right observation of the situation, the action comes up instantaneously and then it is really creative. Otherwise it's more or less a reaction.

So the insight gives you right observation?

I would say, the insight comes from the situation itself, from right observation—attention without selection. It is the art of living in not-knowing, living really in openness. When you live in openness your highest intelligence functions and your personality functions completely differently, because in this openness your whole being acts with the highest sensitivity. In this openness there is absolute security, but of course the person feels in absolute insecurity!

When I look at the human body I see a superb piece of mechanical and physiological engineering, and yet in the course of my work as a physiotherapist I see bodies coming in that are tremendously stressed and strained psychologically. I also see a lot of what I suspect are cases of cancer that might have been psychologically induced by the person's attitude toward life which was formulated over a number of years, the psychological having a profound effect upon the physiological. Is there a possibility that if we as human beings get to know the psychological aspect more, we could eliminate a single great cause of dis-ease—therefore disease—within humankind?

Every illness is a reaction, so it is important for the patient to first accept the illness, not as a concept but as a percept. In accepting it you don't feed the illness any more. Functionally accepting and living with it is the only way to healing. The doctor helps the healing process, and until a certain age the body still has a memory of health, because one is born with health. So, from my experience one must show the patient how to learn to live with the problem of cancer; it is the only way.

So the best thing for them is to totally accept the fact and not move away from it?

Absolutely, absolutely, but not in a fatalistic way. Accept the symptoms, not the idea, not the word. Do not name it "cancer." There was a big conference in Chicago several years ago concerning whether to tell the patient he has a disease or not. Approximately 72% of the doctors said you must tell them, the rest said: Don't tell them. In my opinion one must not name it, because the name is already so conditioned through radio, television and all the papers that the very word "cancer" goes against healing.

You must love it, that is all. When you really love it you will find the way to face it. There must be a certain cooperation. In my experience you must always go from the general to the particular, you must never go from the particular to the general; that is the approach of Hippocrates, from the general to the particular. That means you must face the whole body psychologically and also biologically, because food and all kinds of things play a very important role.

What do you suggest one should do with the fear of illness?

Fear is in your mind. The word fear has a very strong effect in the body-mind. So I would say: Live with this effect in your body-mind; see it from your globality, listen to it, it is compressed energy. Otherwise you are identified with it, and you create it.

And when you live with this and actually see the fear, does it cure the effect?

There is not only one cause, there are many many causes. When you are afraid, have you looked in the mirror at your face? When you are anxious, have you looked in a mirror?

*I*N PURE PERCEPTION *does there come a moment when the observed disappears into a feeling of "I am," and there isn't actually looking any more?*

In the "I am" there is only looking; there is not a looker and no object to look at.

In the feeling of "I am" do you actually see physically the object in front of you?

In the "I am" there is nobody to know "I am." In the moment of pure perception, the perceiver dissolves, and as there is no longer a perceiver, the perceived dissolves too. What remains is only beingness.

"I am"?

Yes.

And then you don't actually see with the eye the object that brought you to the state of "I am"?

The object is in the "I am." It has its homeground, its potentiality, in the "I am;" there is no *object* at all.

So does that mean that if you were established in the state of "I am" you would see no object?

You don't see independent objects any more. You see that the object is an expression of consciousness; you name it, you give it a form, but you see it as an extension of consciousness. But the "I am" is present in the absence of the object; the "I am" never changes. In other words it is the ultimate subject. When you look at an object there is only looking; but when you say later, "I saw the object," you are referring through memory to an image of a person who saw the object. When you say, "I saw," it is a concept. So the real "object" is only there when you are the seeing, because consciousness and its object are one.

Because when the feeling of being is there, I feel there is only that?

Yes.

But sense perception still operates?

Yes.

Could you clarify that a little? I think some people are under the impression that in the "I am" there is a withdrawal of the senses . . .

The "I am" is constantly present. It always is, while the eyes, the ears, the nose and mouth accomplish their functions. That is meditation from moment to moment. Meditation only belongs to the "I," it is not the withdrawing of the senses. I have already mentioned the image of the monkey who closes his eyes, his ears, his nose, his mouth to meditate!

I wonder why we feel the need to fill the silence, to talk, to have some activity, which so often seems destructive to my perception of globality?

We are not describing the ultimate. Words here are symbols to point us to what in reality cannot be talked about. It is tremendously important to hear the words in this way. Do not hang onto the language, do not try to fix it in the frame of understanding. I use words only as pointers. So don't stay with the heard word, but let what is behind the words come to you; then you come to the understanding, and in this understanding you will have a glimpse of *being* the understanding. So our manipulation with words is only to come to the understanding with the right representation. It is here that there is a glimpse of reality. And then this representation, this understanding which is still a formulation, completely vanishes, dissolves in being the understanding, and there is nothing more to understand. When you have discovered listening, non-intentional listening, listening where there is no listener and nothing to listen to, no anticipation and free from all expectation—what we call innocent attention, innocent listening—then there is a transmission. We could simply sit here and not speak. But you must come to the understanding, for it is in the understanding that you have the gift of truth. What you have understood through words are my words; you should understand it with your words. When you find your words in my words, that means you have understood. You should even try to transpose it, make the understanding really clear, as clear as a geometrical pattern. Then you are at the threshold of reality and will have the glimpse. So all that remains to do is to live with this representation. Then one day it will be more than a glimpse; it will be established and you will immediately feel that on waking up in the morning and going to sleep at night and in the interval between two thoughts and two perceptions, you are the background, the "I am." So don't emphasize the object any more, but let the object emphasize the background in which you are constantly.

Dr. Klein, what defines the moment of this supreme awakening?

It is grace. And grace is when you are in your total absence, for this total absence is your presence. You are it now! Perhaps you will discover that you refuse it, you refuse the death of the "I," the "me."

When you have experienced pure perception, rather understandably there is a desire to experience it again, and this desire in a subtle way is extraordinarily strong. I'm beginning to see that this desire keeps the door shut, as it were. The phrase you use—tthis innocent attention—could you tell us more about the quality of this innocent attention?

It is very clear that the desire comes from what you desire and what you desire can never be expressed in thought form; it is unthinkable. But when you become completely attuned to the desire—and you can be sure that when you relax completely you become one with the desire—it brings you to the most desired, which is your openness, which can never be asserted, which is not objective. Openness cannot be compared; it has its own taste. We are very conditioned on the level of our senses. We know the taste of a peach, we know the taste of anything that is eaten, but do we know the taste of our mouth? Have you once tried to taste your mouth? I don't think so! We know only what is objectified, thought of, represented, but we don't know our emptiness.

And that emptiness is the emotional base to the innocence?

When we speak of innocence it means there is no projection, no expectation nor end-gaining. It is really the now. We can never find the now in the head, it is in the heart. Be clear that it can never be fixed, can never be an object. We cannot think of it or represent it.

Seeing beautiful things there is a strong attraction to them. One tries to remind oneself that it is all within, but because of this attraction one actually feels the mind and body contracting into a separation, and there doesn't seem to be a way out, though I feel it has to do with acceptance?

The feeling of beauty in objects comes from your own beauty. You say this object, this picture or this poem is beautiful, but it is your own beauty that you project. Otherwise how could you speak of beauty? It is your own projection.

But that doesn't seem to be enough. There seems to be a desire to participate in the beauty; it might be a collection of happy people, for instance.

The urge to join a collection of happy people may be a certain form of looking for security.

It has that flavor, yes.

When you face a beautiful object and the object points to beauty, it is your own beauty to which it points. When you feel your own beauty stimulated by the object, the object has performed its function and you live in your glory, in your autonomy.

Is the difficulty in listening to the words of truth inherent in the human condition, or are there some societies which have a more immediate access?

The society of the new age will understand that conflict exists only where there is an ego, that living as a person means restricted living. To take yourself for somebody is a restriction; to take yourself for a man or a woman is a restriction. When you take yourself for nothing, then you are in your totality. This way of living is the only way we can speak of a new age.

You talked earlier about learning how to give up. Could you say a little more about that?

When there is tension in our body, it is not to be noted superficially, but to be made an object of our observation. The moment you objectify the tension, you are no longer an accomplice to it. Learning how to give up takes time. When you learn how to give up, you will awaken the organic memory of giving up. Then when you are in society and you react, you will automatically know how to give up in the moment itself, and then face again your surroundings. And there will be a moment when you no longer react.

Are you saying that if there is a reaction in certain circumstances, one cannot face the surroundings without first giving up the reaction?

If you cannot give it up in the living moment, then go home!

Is it necessary to work with the body in order to arrive at truth?

There are many ways to approach truth, of course, but I would say your body is your nearest object. All experiences belong to your body-mind.

Could you say a little more about the new age?

The new age is dimensionless, because our listening, our presence, is dimensionless. Dimensions are directions and belong to the mind; they are still restrictions. Your openness is completely directionless. So the real discovery is to find oneself in this directionlessness, without localization. Here there is only functioning, there is no entity who functions; it is spontaneous living. It would be interesting to try one morning or afternoon to only function, function without reference to your personality, without reference to your experience. Try only functioning and see how this way of behavior acts on you. You already know spontaneous action—those moments in daily life when there is no reference to the already known, when there is no time to remember or reflex to remember, there is only doing. It is something tremendous and beautiful to feel free from the doer and simply be doing.

Why do we always feel we are the doer?

It is only after the doing that you have the habit of saying, "I have done it," so after the doing, it is better to say, "I have been the witness to it but I am not the doer." It may help you to clarify that there is only doing. It is the "me" which attributes the doing to itself. It is a robber. But in the actual doing there is no "I."

I watch my child being so influenced by his peers and school and so on. What can I do to help him not become a clone of society?

You cannot avoid the influence of society. But what is important is that when your behavior is one of freedom with your child, the surroundings have no hold over the child, no power to give the child the idea that he is somebody.

That's intriguing. Could you say a bit more about how to praise the act and not the person, for example? To help them see it more objectively and not to personalize it?

When the child is free from the image of itself, then the child will explore, will inquire. The parents show it how to inquire, how to listen, but never assert what is to be seen, what is to be heard or touched. So one must learn with the child how to inquire, how to explore. This makes the child creative. The child must be free from concepts, from systems. The relationship with the child must be relationless and free from tension. Don't put the child in a frame. In the new age the problem of competition will change also, competition will be eliminated—but that may be more or less wishful thinking!

When you say, "Know your capital," I'm beginning to think that you don't mean something about the past, you mean that this has to be discovered?

Yes, you can only discover your capital from moment to moment, otherwise it is memory.

We have heard you speak about memory, and I take it that living in memory is wrong. Could you speak a little more about this?

You must discover yourself every moment in every situation. To discover yourself, you must be open, there must be no repetition.

Ask yourself why there is repetition. It is because you live mainly in intention. Intention is projection from the past into the future. We live in end-gaining, achievement, so we use memory to project the past into the future. The future is immensely rich but you cannot face that richness because you project the old onto it. In this way you put a wall between you and life, which is actually always new. Go away from the wall. The wall is only living in expectation, anticipation, intention. When you live in intention-lessness, there is life and you live in life; otherwise you live only as an object. Being free from anticipation, being free from intention is free living, and you will discover your childhood and all that life brings to you. That is an experience from moment to moment, there's joy in it—otherwise everything is boring! (laughter)
Thank you.

*C*OULD YOU SAY A WORD *about the kind of food we should eat to try to purify the body and make it more sensitive?*

Be a witness to your psychosomatic function, but don't make the witnessing an action, don't make it something you do. Witnessing is not passive or active, so don't be fixed in it. Become more and more acquainted with your body-mind, how you function in daily life, your reactions, your resistance. It is the awareness of it that brings the change, that brings the purification. But don't make the witness active, for then it is mind, judgment, comparison, inter-pretation.

The spoken words are pointers to the essence that we are. Spoken words are pointers and seeds, which bring you one day to understanding. In the understanding there are glimpses of this reality, and one day the understanding also vanishes in being the understanding. It is only in a very clear mind, where you see the perspective with great clarity, that there are these glimpses. But you must live with your silence, it is only through silence that these seeds unfold. It is a very high art to live with silence and not touch it, not manipulate it with the already known, with memory.

What is mental illness?

It is only in isolation that mental illness comes, and it is only love that frees you from isolation. You must first love yourself; you can never love your surroundings without first loving yourself. I'm not speaking of the body-self.

It seems that one has to spend a lot of time observing oneself and watching one's ego, and I get fed up with myself constantly being the object of my observation.

Yes, but you are making this observation active. Your observation is stuck to the observed. Your observation must not be interested in obtaining something or achieving anything. That is not really observation. Let your observation be completely disinterested.

So when you say ,"Observe yourself," it means being the observation?

Yes, being the observation. The observed appears in your stillness. Observation is stillness.

When there are parts of your body that are not well, how do you work with that? In a global way, or by observing the part?

In your case I would say turn your observation to the parts of your body which are completely healthy and which are not contracted. Become familiar with the feeling of the healthy areas, and from these healthy parts, infiltrate the healthy sensation to the parts which are contracted. It is this organic healthy sensation which brings a kind of rectification of, in your case, your shoulder. Feel it really, and then you may come to the extension of the feeling from the shoulder area to your fingers, elbows, etc. Because when there is some unhealthy feeling, very often there is compensation in other parts of the body which you must detect also. You will discover these compensations through exploration. Feeling sensation and giving-up, letting-go, releasing, go together. If you don't give up completely, the feeling cannot blossom.

How can one keep joy without retaining it as memory?

Joy is causeless; you attribute a cause but it is causeless, so try not to refer this joy to a cause. When you refer the joy to a cause, you insult the Cause! But when you really see it is causeless, it will become very strong in you; it becomes you. When you see it is causeless, in a certain way it grows; but you make it weak when you refer to a cause, because you make a state of it. One day you will be able to go into it knowingly and lose yourself in it; it will be as a background. Freedom, love, peace, are causeless. You cannot put them in the frame of the already known.

Why is it that one may have a moment of freedom from the personality and know that I am nobody, and then in the next moment one is back in the personality again? Does that have to happen many times before the freedom becomes permanent?

Yes, it may happen many times, but every time it happens you must be aware of it, so that you don't identify yourself with it any more. To identify yourself with your personality is more or less a reflex. You must see, when the reflex comes up, that it is a kind of feeling of insecurity; you are looking for a hold.

So there is something that is not quite prepared to accept that freedom?

Yes, because freedom means being free of the person. When you really see that the personality is an accumulation of stuff from your life with which you identify yourself—when you really see it—I would say that is enlightenment. See how the personality acts in the moment when you are free of it; how does your body-mind feel in this freedom? You must completely explore the absence; when you explore the absence, you are in fullness. Otherwise you live fractionally.

When one is perhaps looking at nature and another person comes, the personality comes up to meet them. I don't know how to prevent that.

In looking, there is only looking. So see that when comparison, interpretation, judgment come in, you are no longer related to the seeing. Let the seeing completely unfold, and in this seeing, in this unfolding, you will feel some insecurity, because this looking is not objective, not localized. Looking is really loving the object.

I understand that in order to get beyond my psychological self I have to give up. Then who or what is trying to become happy, or experience joy?

When you live with your surroundings, don't make it a psychological relationship. It becomes psychological the moment it refers to the personality, the person. You know moments when you face situations perfectly and completely without judgment, which don't belong or refer to the psychic "stuff." In these moments you feel whole. In feeling whole there is joy and there is no conflict. But the moment there is choice, the moment there is selection, there is conflict. In choiceless awareness, free from selection, there is not an "I," there is not a "me;" there is global seeing, whole seeing. So it is necessary to familiarize yourself more and more with non-intentional observation, with non-intentional living.

This giving-up—you have said again and again that this is not something we do, it is something which just happens of itself. But I find that my trying to give up just becomes more and more subtle. It's very difficult to leave it alone. Can you help with that?

You said it is difficult, that means that you refer to something which is easy! I would say: Free yourself from the word "difficult" and also "easy;" then you will really see it, because the moment you say it is difficult, you are in the mind which functions in complementarity and is split between "easy" and "difficult." So see it free from the mind, free from the "easy" or "difficult," and then you will really face what is. It is only when you are free from your will, free from volition, that there is a real giving-up. Being free from volition means you do not interfere. It is a passive-active non-state. It is passive in the sense that the "me," the ego, does not interfere, and it is active in that we are completely lucid, completely aware, completely alert and clear to face the circumstances. But be aware, see how it functions when you immediately qualify it as difficult.

How effective are the postures in bringing liberation?

The posture is an archetype. When you do it correctly, it acts not only on the physical plane, but also on the psychological plane. It brings about a reorchestration of the energy. By "correctly," I mean it is the tactile feeling which takes the body into the posture. In other words, the posture is in the feeling, the feeling is not in the posture. First is the feeling sensation, then comes the posture—not vice versa, as usually happens.

The posture must be seen like a picture outside of yourself, outside of your observation; you must be able to transpose this picture in every direction in the space, so that when you are doing it you are not sitting here, you are in the different postures in space. Then you are really sure that you are not involved in the posture. Then you feed the posture, you nourish the posture, with your breathing. In a certain way you are completely a witness and attentive to the posture. Accomplishing the posture is only possible when you are really attentive, when you listen to it. It is an unconditioned listening, free from all expectation. This attention, this listening, refers to itself; so you will find yourself in this listening, free from any localization, either inside or outside. Listening is timeless. What exists is in time and space; what *is*, is timeless.

Certain bodies are more conditioned than others. Can the postures help everyone even if the body is very conditioned, and is it necessary to do them?

In the *Yoga Sutras* of Patanjali concerning the postures and the breathing, it is said that every pose is a posture, that sitting on a chair is a posture, lying down is a posture. But it must be a real lying down, it must be a real sitting on a chair; generally, there is much resistance when sitting on a chair or lying down, even in a bed. It is necessary to explore in order to purify the posture, any posture. But generally when we put our body on the chair there is already resistance somewhere in the ribs, shoulders or stomach.

And the goal is to awaken the energy body, the vital body, the real body, no matter which movement we perform?

Yes.

And as you have shown us, we don't actually need to do the movement with the actual physical body . . .?

Exactly. When we do it with the vital body, that is enough, and it will bring you later to the possibility of actually doing it with the physical body.

So what you do with the physical body is really unimportant, it's what you do with the vital body?

Exactly. You must discover the vital body, you must use it. When you become aware of the superficial body you will feel that there are different layers of the body beyond the most obvious. When you close your eyes for a moment and detect the subtle body, you will realize that your body is not limited by the formation of the skin, of the bone-muscle structure. You will feel yourself expanded. I myself have no idea or sensation of my body being limited. Whether my eyes are open or closed, I am everywhere, expanded in space. I cannot say how many meters or how far this expanded body stretches.

Is the vital body an object?

Yes, it is perceived.

But if it is a little undisciplined, is the closest way to contain it through the breath? Is the breath very much associated with the vital body, and a good way to discipline it?

I use the breath, as we said yesterday, for a spiritual purpose, but you can also use the breath for bringing up this vitality.

But when there is unconscious tension, the breath stops.

The stopping of the breath is a reaction of fear. I would say, listen to the natural coming and going of the breath. What is important, when you do these pranayama exercises, is that you first become aware and listen to the body take itself in charge with the coming and going of the breath. When there is psychological disturbance you will see that this natural breathing is affected. So when you sometimes feel that in letting go of the breath there is a block, a psychological interference, then observe it in the moment when you actually feel it. In this observation without a controller, there is no room for interference and you will see that the breath becomes very slow. When there is fear or anxiety, then your breathing is affected, but relax and exhale completely and you will feel that the exhalation flows into silence. There is no stopping it.

So if we take a deep breath, could we use the breathing to reorchestrate the energy?

Yes, absolutely. When there is fear and nervous tension, this breathing is recommended. But before you direct it in any way, first be aware of the natural flow; that is very important. Then, when you are comfortable with the natural flow, you can later direct the breath.

When I meditate, I feel the localization more in the back of my head, but there is a point in the attention which pulls me from the openness behind to the front again.

Yes, but you should sustain it behind, even though the energy has a tendency to want to strike your brain in front. You must be free from the brain, feel yourself at the base of the skull, expanded in the small brain. When you feel yourself very relaxed, you are free from the left and right brain, free from the energy directed into the formulation of concrete thinking which occurs in the forehead. The energy is still there, the pulsation is still there, but you are still master of this energy and there is no formulation or concretization into thought. And then one day you will see that it has slipped into your heart. The heart is the last door.

When there is meditation, there is no meditator and nothing to meditate on, there is only being. There is no localization at all, no inside or outside, it is completely timeless. One day you may feel only space around you, so be completely with the space, dissolve completely in the space. What is important is to be free from the head. You can see very clearly when somebody is free from the head, and when they are not free from the head. When observing certain sculptures of the head of a buddha or bodhisattva in the museum, you can see immediately when the meditation is still fixed in the head and when the meditation is free from it.

What is the difference between doing the posture with the vital body only and imagining the physical body doing it, or visualizing it?

You *feel* the vital body, it is not imagination. The physical body is a glove, and the vital body goes into the glove. It is the vital body in the glove that makes the glove alive. The vital body is perceived; visualization is a concept.

The energy body is a tactile sensation? And visualization takes place in the head?

Yes. When you go into a dark room and you know there are many obstacles in this room, what do you do? You are not here in your head. You are here and there, moving around the room with your tactile sensation.

I would like to ask about listening referring to itself. For example, if I am sitting in a garden, there is an awareness of looking at a tree, there is an object and there is attention which seems to come from me to the object. Suddenly I hear a bird sing, and the attention switches from the tree to the bird, so how does one move to this state of just seeing, just listening?

When you are in the state of choiceless listening, there is no withdrawing of the senses, the senses are open. There is seeing but there is nothing seen; there is hearing but nothing is heard.

But can the object still be appreciated in that state?

Of course. But the moment you say, "I am writing and the bird disturbs me," it means you have established a personal relationship with the bird!

But in what you call choiceless listening, how does one decide, as it were, whether to listen to the bird or the sound of a jet?

You can only have one object at a given time, you can never have two objects at a given time; but still your ears, your mouth, your nose, your specific organs are open. There is a kind of seeing, but nothing is seen.

So what would attract one to a bird in this multidimensional listening, rather than the sound of a jet? Does one choose?

No. Your ears are open, that is all. But the moment you say, "This bird is singing," you are no longer in non-dual listening. The confusion in many forms of so-called meditation is that, in attempting to destroy the senses by sitting there in apparent tranquility, you create an introverted state which comes when you "meditate" and goes when you are "not meditating." But when somebody is in this background living with open ears and eyes, the bird and all things appear, the meditation is not disturbed by anything.

But can you give some guidance about how one moves from the active sound listened to, to the listening which refers to itself? Or does this just come of its own accord?

There must be first the deep desire to bring the object back to its homeground. Then you spontaneously stop grasping the object. It is the grasping that maintains the object as object. The moment you let go of the emphasis, it dissolves in your listening.

Before this is established, there may be coming and going, but when there is this establishment of your real nature, in your background, there is no disturbance, there is no distraction. The moment it appears as a distraction, then you have established a personal relationship with it.

You said that at a certain moment there is a switch-over when the attention which was eccentric—directed to the flowers—is reabsorbed and becomes concentric—in the seeing itself. How do you come to the threshold so that the switch-over can happen? Do you let go of the focus on the object?

Yes, you release the object, you stop grasping it. Then the object completely unfolds in your awareness. That is why I say that potentially every object points to your awareness.

So you must let it unfold?

Unfold, and then it comes back to you, its homeground.

And to let it unfold you actually have to, in a way, be behind you, and relax?

Absolutely. The energy must be concentric, not eccentric. In reality all energy comes from observing, the stillness, the awareness, tends to return to it. It is only the mind which, through memory, prolongs the duality. But when you let go of projecting the energy and let the object return to you, then every object seen brings you back to the seeing; every object heard brings you back to the hearing. It points constantly to the "I am."

Dr. Klein, could you talk about discrimination? In America two girls were asking you about this because they lived under a freeway which was terribly noisy and they hated living there, so they were asking if they should move or should they accept the noise? When there is no choice, how do you discriminate or decide anything?

Discrimination comes from right observation, it comes from choiceless, non-selective observation. It occurs when you have taken note of all the facts of a situation. You can only see the facts when you are objective, not psychologically involved; otherwise your reactions prevent you from seeing the facts. Included in the facts are your possibilities, your capital, your relations, all that belongs to your existence at this point in time on the planet.

So you see the place is noisy and there is action?

If you establish a personal relation with the noise, you cannot act. But it may appear as a kind of sensation which affects you on the biological level . . .

So you don't have a psychological reaction?

Absolutely not. It is the psychological reaction which is the disturbing factor! (laughter)

But if your body doesn't like it, you may change the place?

Of course. That belongs to biological survival, yes. If you can afford it, you change your flat!

And if you can't afford to move, you accept it completely?

Exactly!

You have spoken of the personality as a tool, and yet personality seems to be the major problem. Could you give an example of how one uses the personality without being attached?

You will use the personality when it is necessary to use the personality, but you will not identify yourself with the personality. You will not see situations, facts, in relation to the personality; you will not be psychically related. Situations appear according to your position. The world in itself is not the problem; what causes the apparent problem is our point of view.

But I find that the personality—when I think I'm not attached to it—still seems to interfere and wishes to change the facts.

See the exact moment you interfere, the precise moment when there is a choice. For you it would be good to sustain your attention, sustain your choiceless observation. Then you will see that this observation refers to itself and you will have a completely new relationship with your surroundings. You will have space around you, because what takes up the space is the psychological interference; it absorbs the space and you are stuck to the situation.

So when I'm involved in some action and I forget myself, forget to remember that it's my wife's birthday and I've got to go home early and I'm still working, am I lost? Or what is that state?

When you say, "I am lost," there is somebody who notes that you are lost!

But I only know that when I come out of it and realize that I haven't gone home when I should have!

I would say for you: Visualize the situation again, but see it from your globality.

When you say to visualize the situation, do you mean at that moment, or afterwards?

Visualize the situation afterwards, but see it from your globality. When you do so, it will have an effect on you in other situations and you will more quickly see them and face them with your globality. In the beginning, you will realize only afterwards that you have been involved in the situation, and then you will see it in the actual situation itself. Then there will come a moment when you see it before the pulsation and identification come up. But of course the absence of the personality creates insecurity. Take note, too, of that insecurity.

I find it very difficult to see the blocks. Could you say something about that?

There are residues in you of anticipation and grasping which hinder you from spontaneous speaking and doing, and you must become aware of these residues. In becoming aware of these residues, they are dissolved. But you must face the residue in its actuality, in the moment itself, because immediately it becomes memory.

I find it very difficult to separate perception and conception.

But the space between perception and conception is merely psychological space. Remain in the perception.

But the reflex to conceptualize happens so quickly.

Yes, it is very quick, so be aware of it. The perception is real, the conception is not real. Conception is memory, it takes you away from the real. Sit on the bench outside and observe the clouds, or the flowers, or the fish, without giving any direction to the fish or any direction to the clouds!

I find that when I meditate, what I thought was stillness is only freedom from activity.

Stillness is not a function. You must awaken in this unfurnished stillness. Discover yourself in stillness, explore the body's stillness. The more you feel the stillness in your body, the more you will feel it also in your mind. This stillness that you first find in the body and the mind is still an object, but this stillness will also vanish in the ultimate stillness. So don't try to localize the stillness, this highest stillness that you are; don't try to be still, because in any case you are still. Your functional nature is stillness; you can only see when you are not still. Don't try to be good, don't try to be wise; your real nature is wise, your real nature is good.

Thank you. I enjoyed being with you!

Provence, France

September 1989

We climb up twisting mountain roads to a high sunburned valley, flanked by chalk cliffs and dotted with pines. In the warm air, wild scents appear: lavender, thyme, rosemary, sage. Objects are not objects, but color and light in space. The country of Cezanne.

La Sainte Baume, an old monastery in need of repair, welcomes us with simple rooms and hearty food. We enjoy our togethereness, the soft dawns and dramatic sunsets, the climb through the dark forest to the grotto of Saint Mary Magdalene high up in the white cliffs. The bell tolls across the valley. Otherwise there are no sounds, no noise polution. An objective silence which echoes the silence within...

L ET US BEGIN AT ONCE. We can open the dialogue.

Monsieur Klein, please, a young woman has just died. She was capable of living meditation, of an aware presence. I don't know how to formulate the question very well, but in which way did she die?

Birth is for someone, death is for someone. The question is: Who is born and who dies. All that is born or dies is the concept "I." When you see it from this standpoint, birth and death have a completely other meaning. Birth is an accident, an accident of two people. The real birth is the birth of "I Am." One must ask oneself very profoundly, "Who lives?" One must free oneself totally from all this secondhand information, for example, that we live our life. In truth we are lived, *it* is lived. We don't choose our birth, death, illness or suffering. The only freedom we have is to become aware of what we are in reality. This is the only freedom we have. There are no other freedoms.

Our only birth is the "I Am," as you say, but can we say that the "I Am" is born?

The "I Am" is permanent. You are awake in the "I Am." You are born at every moment.

Monsieur Klein, my brother committed suicide a long time ago, but even today I ask myself if I can still somehow help him.

You must love him. By love him, I mean be that which you have in oneness, in unity, with him. Be that unity. The dream continues for him. By being one with him I don't mean think of him, but be the non-thinking.

When one asks oneself the question, "Who lives?" we can never find the one who lives. It is an idea, a concept. When that is clearly seen one awakens in life. Then there is only life. Life lives itself. There is perfect spontaneity.

Life expresses itself through our body. We are a channel.

How can we know if we are really living as you say?

When you ask, "Who lives?" you will never find anyone and you will understand that there is no one who lives, that there is only living, only function. The only freedom you have is to awaken in the witness, to be witness of the stage of the world in you. There is no world stage outside you. This witness, this presence, is only in the total absence of yourself, the absence of being somebody. In this absence of yourself, you live plenitude. Otherwise you live only in fraction.

Since this morning I have been witness to my anxiety and agitation. And yet they have not disappeared.

You are taking note intellectually. Taking note means being totally open to what is being taken note of. Let it completely express its secret. Let it be completely articulated. The perceived has its potentiality in the perceiver. And the perceived finds its answer in the perceiver, in the witness, in presence. What is seen can never find its solution in the seen. It can only find a solution in the seer. There are not two, there is only one. The seer and the seen are one. So, pedagogically speaking, I would say bring what is seen to the seer. The seen finds all its expression, its reason for being, its solution, in the looking itself. The looking can never be perceived. It is the ultimate perceiver.

Is this bringing the seen to the seer an act of will or grace?

There is no one who looks, there is only looking. What is seen is only a projection of the looking and finds its home in the looking. But this looking cannot be seen because it is consciousness, presence; it is not objective.

So it's only through a letting-go that this happens?

Yes, it happens by itself. It is one of the elements of *sadhana* that all objects refer to the ultimate subject. This presence is inconceivable, the nearest to yourself; it is not localizable or attainable. To leave here and to go there is a going away from what is the nearest. Even one hair of movement is a going away. All perceived objects have their reality in the ultimate subject, in ourselves, and bring us back to ourselves. This "ourself" is an apperception of our totality.

Sir, you say we are not responsible for our birth or our death, that we are a channel, that there is no one who looks, and so on. You say the only freedom we have is to find our real self. So my question is: Who makes the choice to find this freedom?

What we are profoundly reveals itself by itself. We are the subject of all objects. To think we can direct or fashion our lives as we want, belongs to the dream, to the film. To believe or not to believe also belongs to the film. The only reality is to be the light which illumines the film.

But all the same, Monsieur Klein, when I saw you eleven years ago you gave me a key which I've kept: "observation without judgment." You may say the only thing we can do is to be the light, but you gave me the key and I've kept it. That is still something.

What I gave you was only to understand what you are not. This understanding leads you automatically to feel what you are profoundly.

All objects have their potentiality in the ultimate subject. The subject that is often mistaken for the ultimate subject is also an object. The ultimate subject is beyond subject-object. In reality, subject-object is a concept. When you look at an object, where is the subject and where is the object? There's only looking. It is only afterwards that you talk of subject and object. There is no thought and no thinker, there is only thinking.

What has the yoga practitioner been looking for for so many years?

To get to know the part of you which is not you. You can only say, "I am not the body, emotions and thoughts;" but before saying that you must know what the body, emotions and thoughts are. To know yourself calls for listening, being receptive, open. In this opening all refers to yourself. If you are completely open to the expressions of life, they refer to life, because they are only life and nothing else. So when you learn what you are not, you are learning what is an expression of yourself. And, pedagogically, it is better to go this way; to investigate first what you are not, to understand profoundly what it is that you are not. And it is important to do this in the moment itself. When fear and anxiety appear, when hate and all the feelings appear; see them on the field, in the moment they occur. You have to be alert and open, and at a certain moment the openness will refer to itself. Because what you are fundamentally is only openness. Openness is not an object, it is quite simply emptiness, empty of objects, a question mark. So you cannot affirm what you fundamentally are. If you do, you make it an object and it belongs to what you are not.

You say there is no subject who looks, there is only looking . . .

There is only looking. Any "I looked" or "I saw this" is a concept.

I agree, but can we not say that if we are not aware of this looking, it is lost, that it depends on our awareness?

In the moment itself there's only listening, only looking. Consciousness and its object are one, not two. Later you make it two.

If I say I am the light of life, I have made it an object, so is it only in formulating it that it is lost?

Yes, before the formulation, you are. Because peace, love, joy cannot be put into any formulation.

What are mantrams for?

Mantrams have no importance in their content, only in their pronunciation. One must pronounce all the different vowels and sounds perfectly, dental, labial, guttural and so on. In each vowel is a different localization. It takes a lifetime to pronounce it as it must be pronounced. If you pronounce it as it must be pronounced, then it strikes certain parts of your body which are completely out of tune and not functioning. In the reorchestration of these energies, you may come to what you are profoundly. But you don't need a mantram to be what you are profoundly.

When the sound, which is perceived, is impersonal and dies in the silence, can it lead us to our real silence?

When you are living in your absence, a chord which is in vibration is capable of putting your chord in vibration. This is what we call the transmission. There is nothing else to transmit. Real transmission is the transmission of vibration, to strike your chord, light your flame. Your silence in this moment is alive, but it is beyond all subject-object, all "I am silent." It cannot be localized.

Does this justify the theory that the tradition was perhaps oral?

Yes. But what is pronounced orally must be actual. One doesn't transmit doctrines, four, eight, nineteen hundred years old, but the actual, present essence of the tradition. One must live the essence in order to be able to formulate it in present language, and so transmit it.

There is then a very big difference between being a witness in silence and silence without a witness.

The witness is, in any case, silence. It is not an object. As long as there is duality, the witness is objective. But when the reflex to take yourself for a person has completely left you, the witness disappears also and there is only consciousness. The witness is only an extension of consciousness and when the reflex to be someone disappears, then the witness disappears.

Can the reflex to take oneself for a person be perceived?

Absolutely, you know it very well! And sometimes you even smile when you see it appear. But one day it has no more role to play, and it will leave you. First you ignore it, then you forget it. In any case, the day comes when you *must* forget it and if you can't forget it, you will not pass on happily!

This morning you said attention is silence. I don't completely agree, so perhaps I have not understood. It seems to me that in an aesthetic state there is a moment of expansion and dilation where there is no attention. Am I wrong?

But when you live this moment of expansion, it is a perceived object. You perceive it.

I feel it.

You perceive it. So there is still subject-object relationship, but when this expansion is not formulated, is not conceptualized, it stays in pure perception, a direct perception. Then the perceived dies in the perceiver and there remains only presence-attention.

This fusion can only happen when you are free from the mental; free from judging, comparing, evaluating, and so on.

If I have understood well, you just said that the reflex to take oneself for a person disappears when there is no more reason for it to exist; but what is its reason for existence in the first place?

In everyday life you may see very often how there's only action, only spontaneity. You know these moments. You know moments too when your action is only intentional. When there is intention there's the "me;" otherwise, there is no "me." In living in anticipation, no spontaneity is possible.

But what is the function of this "me"?

It is only a fabrication you have made yourself.

But we did not choose to make it.

You formulated it, built it with the help of society, your experiences.

So it does have a function?

It has only a conceptual existence. It is an object which you perceive.

What use does it have?

This object is full of anxiety.

But what is it for?

It is for nothing.

Why create it then?

It has no purpose. It is a complete illusion. But when you see this clearly, when you see it is an object, ask, "Who is seeing it?" Then there is a letting-go. When this letting-go is completely profound, it reveals your light, your clarity. The moment you really see that what you think you are is pure construction, then there is illumination. That is awakening, the real awakening.

So see that you live all your life with a personage that has no reality, that chooses, refuses, suffers, that lives constantly between the yes and the no, the positive and the negative, sympathy-antipathy, joy-suffering. Ask yourself who knows all these opposites, positive and negative. Who?

The other evening I was listening to Mozart and I felt a great joy, a bliss, I would even say. Was this sentimentality, or the ultimate joy you talk about?

225

There were moments when Mozart lived this joy and could transmit this joy through sound. There are certain of his works where you feel this joy. I'm not speaking of those works which are stained by a worldliness. I'm talking about those works which are expressions of his joy. Not the joy of Mozart but joy itself. When you listen to them they lead you to your joy. Because music, sound, is a supreme object to lead you to what you are fundamentally. All objects lead you to your real nature, it is the nature of the object; but some are more pointers than others.

If I say I am looking at something, I am no longer in the looking, so. . .

When you look, there is only looking.

And my question is . . .

And when you say, "I look at this flower" there is only the concept, flower. When you say, "It is I who looked," there is only the personage that you think saw it.

That's right. The question I want to ask is: What is the point of saying, "I looked at something" other than to maintain the person?

When the looked refers to the looking, there is nobody.

Yes. But that . . .

In the looking there is no one, there is only looking. In listening there is only listening. There is no one who listens and no one who looks.

But does the looking know itself as looking?

Yes. Yes. But *you* can never see the looking because you are it.

But if saying "I saw this" maintains the person, then one should never say it.

When you look at something and you memorize what you saw—and all is memory since at the moment of looking there is only looking—so when you say, "I looked at an object" it proves that there was a witness who saw; otherwise how could you say, "I saw the flower." So say rather, "I was witness to this act," but never say, "I saw it." That is important.

One day you said, "The seeker will one day find the sought." Since I have known you, I thought that when I observed my thoughts and emotions, it was the witness observing them. Then one day I dropped all that observing, because I realized that it had brought me nothing, and now I see that it was still the person who was observing. But now it seems I am observed by another quality of looking and I take myself now for the object observed, for the person. So I still feel myself identified with the person, but I have the feeling of being observed. And can this transfer bring me to the real looking, the fact of allowing oneself to be observed? I don't really know where I am at the moment . . .

Innocent looking is your real nature. You are it.

I believe you, but I don't feel I have discovered it yet.

But you cannot take note that you are this innocent looking. You can only take note that you are not it. So see that at certain moments when you analyze, interpret, you are not the innocent looking, that is enough. Because originally you are this innocent observation.

I believe you, but I don't feel I have really profoundly experienced the detachment from the subject-object relationship. And I noticed that the very first time I met you, I received everything and since then there has been an elimination but nothing new.

An object can only become purified, transformed, if it is in reference to the ultimate subject, the innocent observation.

Thank you.

OUR REAL AUTONOMY, our essential nature, is the nearest to us, it is ourselves. Each step to attain it takes us away. This understanding brings all the energy for wanting to attain or be to a state of rest. What we are fundamentally cannot be fixed, cannot be apprehended or attained. We are the ultimate subject which can never be objectified, because it is beyond space and time. We cannot perceive or conceive it. We can only live it in our openness. We can feel this openness in daily recall. We should bring all that is conceived and perceived back to our presence.

Let us dialogue.

Monsieur, is it possible to have aspiration without tension?

This aspiration refers to what? To being oneself. To be oneself comes only from being oneself and in being oneself there is no tension. When something refers to our psychosomatic nature there is tension. In your profound desire to be yourself there is no tension. The desire to be oneself comes from what is desired; otherwise, there is no desire. There are not many desires, there is only one desire which embraces all desires and that is to be free, to be autonomous, to be totally oneself.

Then all aspiration disappears?

Yes, and then only one desire remains: to be oneself. To come to this one desire you must see all the other desires and how they are evasions, dispersions, compensations. That must be noted. You may ask yourself what is the motive for all these various desires. You will find there is only one desire: to be autonomous, to be really yourself. When you recognize this, all the other compensatory desires disappear and there is only the one desire left. So at first there is dispersion, then one asks very deeply the question: What am I looking for? And once it is seen that all the dispersions are only a compensation, then you are oriented. To take your word, your aspiration is oriented towards the essential. This aspiration comes directly from what is aspired to; what you desire comes from the desired. Then you must be completely attuned to this aspiration. Be one with it. It is an original feeling which leads you directly to what you desire: being, to be.

Is "to be oneself" a state or an ultimate goal?

Don't have a goal. When there is understanding, in other words, when you feel this oriented aspiration very profoundly, I would say the goal dissolves. There is no more goal. A goal is tension. What is important is that you see how much energy you disperse in your life trying to be autonomous, to be being. All these different directions waste your energy, they make you promises but when you live them they don't keep their promise. They cannot fulfill your desire to be. When you realize this, then only one desire remains.

What is your attitude towards suicide?

Who commits suicide? Suicide is the I-concept. And as this I-concept has no reality, who commits suicide? One must realize that one has identified with this "me" who wants to commit suicide, one has identified with a non-reality. The deep understanding that it is only a fantasy to take oneself for a personal entity is liberation.

May I explain myself more clearly?

Yes, I'm waiting for more precision from you.

The question would be that it seems like an opportunity in situations where there is only escape, fear, anger.

Fear, anger, concern only an object, a "me."

This is clear to me in a moment of meditation, but in the actual moment of daily life, no.

In the moment when fear, anxiety and hate appear, refer immediately to the position of the one who sees these things. Bring them back to yourself. It is you who are the knower of fear and anxiety. Then the energy you put on fear and anxiety is transferred to their knower. This is not a concept. It is an awakening, an awakening in clarity. This awakening brings transformation.

How can one know clarity?

Look at the situation again and see from your clarity what brought fear and anxiety. Don't look at it from the "me" but from your totality, your presence.

But that already asks that one is in a high state, capable of stopping in a situation which is rolling on.

Practically speaking, you have to refer at once to your body instrument, leave alone ideas of fear and anxiety. Only stay with the perception, the sensation. Let it live. Do not feed it with thoughts. Contemplate the perception with very great tranquility.

But that is the problem, how to be tranquil at that moment?

You know moments of crisis. Of course in the middle of a crisis you cannot do very much, but you are not always in crisis. There are moments in the day when you can have a true relation with your body, *la d'étante*, attention without intention.

How can one open to this lucidity in these moments?

When you are not in the crisis, refer constantly to the knower, the ultimate subject, your totality. (long pause) The dreamer is part of his dream. He is the same substance as the dream. To want to get out is to turn in a vicious circle. When you see the process very clearly you are outside it. Then one finds oneself only in presence.

Why does one who has realized his real nature continue to help others?

It is inherent in the realization of one's real nature to become completely integrated in human society. It is not to become a professional helper, one just helps for the love of helping. There is not the slightest intention to help. Simply one's presence is help.

And if everyone were well?

When you have joy in you, it is inherent to joy to share with others.

Sometimes I have the tendency to believe that a life full of suffering, passion, joy is more interesting than when it is beautiful all the time.

But you know the joy and suffering in you. They appear from time to time in a discontinuous manner, but there is a presence in you that one could call love, which is always behind suffering and joy.

To attain the state you are talking about, does it involve effort and work or does one just wait and, well, one day it just happens?

We made it clear at the beginning that there is nothing to attain, nothing to find. When you make the slightest effort you go away from it. Because what you are looking for is not objective. All you can find is an object. The subject—you are it. If you understood this, it would immediately give you a complete letting-go. You would then find yourself spontaneously in a waiting without waiting for anything.

I will ask the question from the other end. What can one do to realize that there is nothing to wait for?

You have without doubt known moments in your life when you said, "I don't know." When you said, "I don't know" there was no more knowing possible. And there was a complete abandonment of knowing anything. Live these moments totally, these moments of letting go of any possible knowing, because in these moments you are open. The openness refers only to itself. It is its own knowing. It does not need an intermediary to know itself. Live completely this "I don't know." Live it without restriction. Give all your attention, give all your love to this "I don't know."

I have the impression that whether I see something totally or partially does not depend on me. I live as I live and it has nothing to do with will.

The moment you say, "I don't know," there is no more reference at all to yourself. When there is no more reference to yourself then you wake in your absence. In the total absence of yourself there is presence.

But when I say, "I don't know" it is not enough because I don't really accept completely that "I don't know." There is still a hope to know. It is not an "I don't know" with my heart. In myself I say ,"I don't know but I really want to know." But you are speaking of an "I don't know" where I don't look any more to know, where there is a total impossibility of knowing. Is that right?

First of all, you cannot know anything that you don't already know. And in what you already know, there is no solution. All that you already know has brought you here to this chair.

Then ask yourself deeply what current brought you to this chair, what motive, what pulsation . . .

It is the cosmos. It is just like that. I was not responsible for coming. Something just brought me here.

And what is this thing that brought you here?

(silence)

You don't know. Well then . . . begin there.

(break)

When one finds oneself closed in a universe of ideas, beliefs, secondhand information, and we find ourselves supremely uncomfortable in this universe; we want to get out by all means. We study books, science, techniques. We go to see this person and listen to that person, all to get out. We try teaching what we have learned, and all this is because we feel profoundly uncomfortable. Then at a certain moment, a maturity occurs and instead of spending our energy reading, studying, visiting, trying to escape, we explore the very desire to get out. We explore the elements which oppress us. We take note that the one who was trying to get out of this universe belongs to the universe. What happens then? There is a stop. This stopping creates the ground for awakening. We find ourselves outside the process. There, transmutation is possible.

We accept, we take for granted, an enormous number of ideas; for example, the belief that we have been born. It is all only secondhand information. There is no proof that you were born. You have accepted unquestioningly that you are a person. And you live your life according to the desires of this person. But when you look more closely you will see you are led.

Can you talk more about what you mean by the word "transmutation"?

The psychosomatic substance finds its transmutation as soon as this substance refers to knowing, to being. It is only presence, the light in us, that allows the transformation of this psychosomatic nature. By transformation I mean harmonization, integration. Up to a certain point our conditioning remains. We are biologically conditioned by our language, our collectivity, our endocrine glands, and so on. We are conditioned by many things. But all this, all we are not, refers harmoniously to what we are. All that we are not must, at a certain point, be forgotten. If we don't forget it, the dream continues. The dream follows.

Physical manifestations that we call fear, can these be without object at a certain moment?

As long as we believe we are a person there will be fear. The person is the ground for fear. The "me" needs situations to exist. Outside the situation it has no existence.

So there is no fear without object?

Absolutely.

Then what do people mean when they speak of metaphysical fear?

This still refers to the I-image, the fear of disappearing. The "me" prefers the worst situation, the very worst, rather than not to exist.

On the subject of transmutation, certain authors have spoken of the biological mutation of the cells. The harmonization of which you speak, could it resemble a biological mutation?

The cell knows its reality. It knows its origin, its own knowing. It is in the very great letting-go that it comes back to its original nature.

It knows its origin but it is full of impurity? Does it have the inner tendency to seek for the purity of its origin?

It has been badly treated, badly used, badly raised. It has been abused, violated by our way of living.

Pardon me, Monsieur Klein, in the real awakened non-state, is there still the memory of the previous, illusory sleeping state?

In your awakened state, all follows its course, but you live in your glory. This awakening is the real birth. The other so-called birth is an accident. But when there is awakening you cannot speak any more of an accident because this "accident" gave you the possibility to be.

I would like you to tell me how much time is necessary for transmutation.

Transmutation happens the moment all your life is seen from the ultimate, the moment all your life refers to your real nature, to consciousness, to presence. Because you see your life, your expressions, in a completely different way. You see them from your globality. When you see your life from your globality, nothing can appear problematic.

Your life which surrounds you, when it refers to your wholeness, takes another form completely because you see the *facts*, not from a point of view, but from the global view which has no point of view. Things don't change, they are what they are; but your way of seeing appears like change, like a transmutation. There is nothing to change. Only your vision can change. And in the right vision is right action, spontaneous action.

Vision, seeing, is always correct when there is no conceptualization. The subject-object division appears only when there's conceptualization. Perception is always correct. It refers directly to seeing, hearing. There is no interpretation.

Thank you very much.

WHEN YOU ARE NOT INHABITED BY ANY OBJECT, then there is plenitude. At that moment there is no one and there is no object which refers to the plenitude. There is only plenitude. It is a word which you cannot put in a mental frame. It is your absence. When you have moments like that you must withhold from naming or qualifying them; otherwise, you make them again mental, conceptual.

Monsieur Klein, is the awakened state perturbed by love or does love precede the awakened state?

Humility and simplicity open the way of love, because in humility and simplicity there is nobody. There is only listening, only opening.

Would you talk about karma?

Karma and reincarnation belong to the world of dreams. As long as you believe in them, the dream goes on. For whom is there karma? Don't answer at once, but delve in yourself for this entity who is submitted to karma.

Does it belong to the great illusion?

Absolutely. It is an evasion, an obstacle preventing you from asking very deeply of yourself: Who am I?

Monsieur Klein, one speaks of karmic illness, what happens to this in the wakened state?

Don't attribute a story to illness. That is still an obstacle to acceptance, to total acceptance, total surrender. It is a justification. The healing and the solution are found in acceptance, not in interpretation.

You have said many times that to understand our real nature, we must be worthy. But doesn't the idea of worthiness belong to the person? Consciousness does not distinguish worthy or unworthy, because everything is a manifestation of consciousness. So isn't it an obstacle to think about being worthy or not worthy?

You must be apt to receive it.

But it is not the person who receives, it is receiving itself. So who is worthy?

You can say worthiness without attaching it to a person. Worthiness is there when you are ready to receive.

So when the idea of worthy or unworthy disappears you are worthy?

Absolutely. The word worthy is a bit tainted with morality, it is true. I use these words sometimes, but being worthy means being ready to receive.

Monsieur, if there is no reincarnation, all the Indian tradition must be invention.

Reincarnation is an Indian way of thinking. It belongs to a very superficial layer of Indian thought. Things are much more complex and more simple than that. But before all, ask who is the entity who is going to reincarnate? You will never find it. When you don't find it, then you will awaken to what you really are. It is the same in meditation. You must delve deeply in yourself to find the meditator. When you don't find him, then meditation stops, all seeking stops and what remains is a kind of current, a current of presence, a current of love.

Is this karmic story an illusion?

I never say yes or no. *You* must find out who reincarnates. Look into yourself and one day you will find yourself in a state of admiration, because when you find nothing you will abandon everything and you will be left in admiration, in astonishment. Then there is nothing to admire, only admiration.

Can you say what you mean by "delve into yourself"?

Interrogate, ask questions. Not questions from books or secondhand information but questions that come from your life. You can be sure you will find the answer, because when you ask the question it is already the answer. The questioner is the response. The question comes from the answer itself. It is not a formulated answer but a lived answer.

You said to me yesterday, "Refer to the knower." Is that the subject of the question? Yesterday I spoke of perturbed emotions and how to practically, in the situation, be in contact with the ultimate reference. For example, this afternoon I took your suggestion from yesterday and went into the forest and tried to feel myself walking.

That is another thought. You have superimposed a pattern of behavior but that's only a new thought.

I'm explaining myself badly . . .

You asked a question yesterday and when you ask it today, it's a new thought. It is not memory. You put a ticket on yesterday.

If you want. I tried to live in this direction.

All that is perceived needs a perceiver, but the perceiver can never be perceived.

This morning when practicing the yoga, when we were in the perception, the knower was there.

When you ask deeply, "Who is the knower?" and find it has no objective existence, there is a stop. You are, for one instant, free from representation, without object. It is a lived moment, perfectly non-dual. Don't try to localize it, to find it in you, because it is simply you. There is no knowledge and no knower. It is not a perception nor a conception. It is a state of being in the total absence of yourself. You know moments in your life where there is no thinking, when you live your absence. It is only in this absence that there is presence. In other words, you can only say "I am" when you have the deep experience of what you are not. The "I am not" precedes the "I am." This can only be lived. In other words, it is plenitude.

I cannot refer to this lived.

You identify yourself with something you are not. When you ask the questions, "Who is the ultimate knower? What is subjectivity?" then you free yourself from the known, the knowable. You must discover the immensity of not-knowing. Real knowing is in not-knowing, because there is no representation. It is experience without an experiencer. So live the tranquility, the vibration, the sonority of the tranquility. Tranquility is only sound and vibration. The concept of tranquility has no place. When you are totally in listening to this sonority you are attuned. It is a moment of unity.

It is the first time I have done the body exercises with you and I wonder if you can tell me what you mean by "feeling" and "sensation."

Your body is seen, heard, felt, touched, but above all it is sensation; it is felt. It is composed of a certain number of layers of sensations, a hierarchy of sensations. You have the superficial sensation first; but even this is usually hidden, veiled by muscular reaction. So this sensation is very rarely declared. When you evoke the tactile sensation, this tactile sensation absorbs the muscular reaction. Then you will discover other very sensitive layers of feeling, of

240

sensation. So instead of working with the physical, neuromuscular body, we work with the energetic body.

When you discover the different levels in your body, it becomes elastic, empty, energized. The body work only has value if you work in this way; otherwise, it is mechanical. It is only this feeling, this sensation, that can transform the muscular structure. The muscle is there but functions badly. When the tactile feeling awakens in the muscles, they function differently. There is the agonist and antagonist functions. The antagonist closes and the agonist opens; but these movements are generally much too exaggerated, excessive, which paralyzes the sensitivity of the skin. So the work by the sensation transforms the muscular structure. This is the only *raison d'être* for the body-work.

Monsieur, how can we attain silence?

You cannot attain it. You are it. Only see what is not silent in you.

Should we practice attention?

Only see what is not silent in you. The easiest way is by facing your body.

You say often "take note" of the perception. What do you mean by "take note"?

It means, feel the nervosity completely; feel what is not tranquil on the neuromuscular level. Contemplate it and in the contemplation it will no longer be fed. There are parts, the chest, the throat, the neck, which are constantly in reaction.

The body has an organic memory. When you have once been in the decontracted state, this organic memory remembers you. See what is constantly in reaction, in activity. Refer very often to the organic memory of relaxation.

But it is very difficult to practice this in everyday life with work, problems, family, and so on.

241

You must be open to the newness of life. Simply open and you will act according to this openness.

You have always a carrot before you. See how you function. You are never without a carrot. Take note of it. Keep a few moments free in the morning to observe yourself. Don't always repeat yesterday. Observe yourself as you look at fish in an aquarium, as you look at children playing. Your life is full of newness. You can only see this from an open mind, a mind not occupied by anticipation.

Monsieur Klein, are there any essential questions we should ask ourselves?

Of course there are essential questions. For you I would say, ask yourself profoundly the motive for your actions. Begin with a burning question: What is my real motive in coming here? What was the state preceding the decision to come here? Was it a lack, an incompleteness in you, and you thought you would find completeness here? You thought that perhaps I could fill your lack? To come here took some effort. You had to take a train, a car, a plane. You had to pay a lot to come here. You could have avoided all that. All of that effort, energy and money spent is thrown out of the window! When you have seen the lack in you, then live completely this lack. Live completely this insufficiency, this lack of fulfillment. Don't just reason it, live with it. In contemplating it this way, the light will awaken in you.

One must see one's motives for actions in the actual moment itself and then pose the question. Only in the actual moment of acting will you find the answer. Otherwise, you go from compensation to compensation. I'm not saying it was entirely a compensation to come here, but you may have had an insight with less effort!

When you really face your lack, you will be out of the conflict, out of the vicious cycle. This "you" which is outside the circle cannot be objectified, cannot be conceptualized. It is a presence that is completely out of the conflict. In contemplating your lack in this way, your contemplation will become more and more relaxed. There will be a space between your contemplation and your lack.

Then I guarantee that your observation, your contemplation, will refer to itself. It is its own knowing without need of an intermediary to be known. This moment must be lived totally. Then, only then, is change possible.

You said to someone that she would act according to her perception. What is the difference between that and reacting to whatever happens to us?

You must understand in the moment itself what is an action and what is a reaction. In our life we generally only know reactions, because everything that happens to us is seen by the "me," the personal point of view. This leads to reaction.

But when you find yourself in contemplation, observing the facts, nothing escapes you, because your looking is not fractional, it is global. Then the fact gives rise to action and this action belongs completely and appropriately to the situation. There is nothing personal in the action, there is no choice in it. It is perfectly adequate, aesthetic, ethical and functional. Anything else is destructive.

Then whether and how to act or not-act is not a kind of bartering. Whether to do one or the other comes from discerning the situation in us. It is not a question of mental bargaining.

Can one know when one is closer to one's real nature?

As long as it is perceived it remains a state you enter and leave and try to maintain. The silence that is our real nature is the totality. No one is silent and nothing feels silent. There is only tranquility beyond all subject-object relationship. This silence appears between two thoughts, two actions. It is expressed in deep sleep. You may discover it in these moments and one day it becomes constant, the light behind all objectification, our background. It is the tranquility of all human beings.

Monsieur, if you please, I would like to reply to what you were saying earlier about the real motive for coming here.

My life just before coming here was as follows: at four o'clock I left the office feeling a bit tired and disgusted, not really feeling part of the office world. I came here, put down my suitcase feeling at home, and I thought, it's too easy to feel this. How can I resolve these two worlds?

When you work in your office and you finish work and go home and say, "I am disgusted with all these activities," it means quite simply that you have established a personal relation with these activities. Tiredness and disgust come only when you are completely identified with your personality. It is the person, the object, which is tired and disgusted, not the "I." In any case, you have to earn your living, face your financial problems. You cannot refuse it. It belongs to your life. But work is only function. There is only functioning. Don't create a personal relation. This creates the fatigue. There is, of course, such a thing as muscular fatigue, but generally what we call being tired is psychological. So go to the office, see the job to be done. See what it needs in order to be realized, but don't establish a personal relationship with it. Then you are witness to your activities, they function, they are done; but you are not drowned, not implicated, not identified with them. In this disidentification you will find joy, because you will be outside all the activities. So never refer your office work to you. What is you is empty, empty of all personage. In this emptiness, plenitude is found. At first, you may feel yourself the witness of your activities, but when they no longer refer to you, you will awake in your absence and in this absence there is no witness, only presence and the joy of living. I assure you.

*O*NE DAY YOU SAID *that the clown is always ready to appropriate the applause of the dancer. What can one do so that that does not happen?*

When the concept "me" appears, take note of it. Automatically, it will stop. So when every action is accomplished, do not attribute it to you. Take yourself not as the actor but as a witness to it. When you stop taking yourself for the actor, the old record that repeats "I am the actor" will be erased, because it has no longer a role. You are the witness of all that occurs on the world stage, but in no instance are you the doer. In the actual moment of an action the idea of being a "doer" doesn't even appear, because two events or thoughts cannot happen simultaneously. When there is action and the "me" comes up, it interrupts the action. If you are skiing and you think "I am a skier" you'll fall in a ravine. For there to be action or art, the actor or artist must disappear.

So you think that to be an artist, the artist must disappear?

When the artist executes what he has conceived instantly in a moment of dream or wakefulness, he does so in space-time. There is only execution, but no executor.

Does the inspiration come only from a global vision or can there be partial vision which becomes fuller in the doing?

The intuition is always global. One must keep this globality knowingly during the execution of it in space and time. When one loses this globality in the execution, then very often one cannot continue.

Then if one sees that one has lost it, can the thought that one can find it allow us to find it again?

Yes, you can find it again, but it must be maintained in the execution. You see yourself how many paintings in the history of painting are left unfinished in the studio. They aren't left unfinished because the artist didn't have the time or money to finish them, but because he lost the feel of the globality, the totality. He lost his vision.

Sometimes, in daily life, when I see my attention is partial and I think "I am in fraction" my attention becomes global.

It is a thought which directs you towards globality, but this thought is not globality, it is only a symbol.

Has this symbol the power to lead me back to globality?

Absolutely. Very often when we lose the feel of globality—you love music and you see for yourself that there are many compositions of even Bach or Beethoven that are not finished. And even in Schubert's famous Unfinished Symphony, there's something missing. He lost the feel. The global feel is a sensation, even an emotion.

What is friendship?

When two people meet themselves in the other, it is a meeting of love; and when there is a sonority, a vibration that stimulates your own sonority, your own sound, then there is friendship. Friendship is on the plane of the personality, on the relative plane, but love is beyond the personality. You may love your neighbor but he is not necessarily a friend. There is a difference.

And why then is there so much violence in our society?

Violence is a reaction to situations that are not convenient for the person. So according to his nature and temperament the person reacts and this reaction is violence. There are many kinds of violence, as you know. Sometimes, however, what appears as violence to another is not necessarily violence. The deception of another may bring an action that is apparently violent but it is not "the person" who is being violent; it is the god in you who manifests in that form. But violence is a reaction.

Can you talk about the meaning of mental illness?

One who identifies with his personality already creates an illness. That's how illness begins. (pause)

Let us respect a silence between the answer and the next question. The verbal answer must be reabsorbed in not-knowing. The answer is knowing but this knowing must die in silence, so let us leave time for this.

Good. Now what is the question?

What is in the heart of a woman? (an Italian asks)

In the heart or the body? (*le coeur ou le corps?*)

(laughter) The heart.

Are you saying, "Does a woman have a heart?"

No, he is saying, "What is in the heart of a woman?"

Ah! Love!

Love?

Yes. Love. *Solamente amore.*

And when this love does not express itself?

Love must not be expressed. Love which expresses itself is not love. When you express love, you objectify it, make a state of it. Love is. Don't try to understand it in the frame of thought. But take note, it is love that is in the heart of a woman!

247

But, yes . . .

But it is still the case that we live in a man's world.

Is there a difference between a man and a woman?

There is no difference. There is a difference between the male and the female, but there is no difference between a man and a woman. But the biological difference is completely effaced in love. The apparent difference is unified.

Do all desires come from the ego?

Desires may apparently come from the ego, but the ultimate desire is certainly to be autonomous, global, fulfilled, and this desire comes directly from what you desire. So, on the most profound level, you desire the desireless state, to be free from all desire, to be fulfilled. When you have found the desire to be, for which every other desire is a compensation, this desire, this emotion should be sustained in you. You must live with this desire. It will lead you to the source of the stream, because the admirer comes from the admired and the admired dissolves completely in admiring and then there is neither admirer nor admired, there is only admiration.

It is a very great art to live with this emotion. Above all, do not interpret it or manipulate it. You must have a certain veneration for this emotion, this desire. Approach it with a feeling of sacredness.

Monsier Klein, if you please, the word memory has several qualities, individual, collective, cosmic, psychological. Would you tell me what you mean by memory in the singular?

When one has completely explored memory, one can say there is no memory. When we say, "I was here three years ago," it is a present thought. The three years is a label only. That you can say, "I was here three years ago" proves that you are the witness. To be the witness of something is not a function. Two functions cannot exist together. This is from the ultimate point of view, of course.

248

Otherwise, everything is memory. We only think in memory. It is something very different if thought comes from silence; then it is altogether creative. But if thought arises in thought, as it usually does, then it is memory, psychological memory. By psychological, I mean it maintains the "me," the person.

I don't believe in cosmic memory. What is "cosmic" memory?

The moment when the cosmos expresses itself through you.

This isn't memory.

All that can be thought manifests in silence. All thought, collective, individual, comes from the total memory—universal, if you prefer. It is not personal.

The notion of memory belongs with the notion of time.

Time appears with thinking. When there is no thinking there's no time.

Between each thought there's an interval as between a tick and a tock on the clock. Here surges up the glory of the present, of presence. There is no absence of tick and tock. Tick-tock creates time and the background of time is presence. Generally we judge these moments as merely an absence of activity, but they are presence, not an objective presence but our presence. It's like the screen in the cinema which is always the same though the film may change every day. What is between two thoughts, two states and in deep sleep is the screen at the cinema.

What is real spontaneity?

Spontaneity cannot be thought. There is only spontaneity in the absence of oneself. In a humble, simple nature there is spontaneity. When a situation doesn't refer to you, when all your actions don't refer to a "you," then there is spontaneous function because there is no intention, no goal, no result you are looking for.

Are events linked to each other and is there a significance between them? Or is it arbitrary?

There is nothing arbitrary in events. We qualify certain events as good or bad, but in reality there are neither good nor bad events. They all refer to the whole.

I had a dream last night that struck me, that my father, who is dead, returned and asked me certain questions. I wondered what you thought of this kind of dream?

One mustn't reason a dream from the waking state. One cannot understand a dream from the waking state. Practically speaking, I'd say live with the emotions the dream produced in you and don't look for interpretation.

Can one consider suffering as a gift?

It depends how you interpret suffering. Suffering is a pointer. Suffering refers to joy and joy to suffering. Suffering cannot exist without joy and vice versa. So to understand these two one must be beyond them. Who knows suffering knows also joy. One must be knowingly the knower. In other words, suffering points to the ultimate subject, the one who knows it. Only an object can suffer, the ultimate subject—never. So, be the subject.

I don't say there is no suffering at all. Simply be the subject. You will find then a distance between you and the suffering and it will lead you to its real meaning.

There is a saying that says, "If you want your dog to become bad, confine him." Is it the same for a human being?

When you take your neighbor for someone, you do so because you take yourself for someone. When you take your neighbor for someone, you imprison him and the person will react. Be free from yourself and you will see freedom in the other, because then there is no other, there is only love. Otherwise, one who is bound binds others.

Is it true that the guru is a mirror of the inner guru?

But life is the mirror. Life is the best mirror that exists.

For one year I have practiced that when I see a thought appear I leave it to go into the infinite space. I feel it has sanctified my life. But when I am in a crucial problem I cannot do this. But since I have been hearing you over the last few days, I have the impression that I delve even deeper into myself. But there is a deep laziness in me and a fear and I see it and am witness to it.

In any case, before going to sleep in the evening, offer up all your qualifications until you find yourself in complete nakedness. Offer all you are not. There is no entity to offer to, only offering. Offer all your thoughts, tensions, qualifications, objects. Then you will sleep in your total absence which is presence.

When you, one day, find yourself at the threshold of relative death, this is the only gesture left to you, to offer all you are not. And not only to offer, you must offer the offering, you die towards the offering and then forget the offering; and then what is left is your light, your clarity, your absence.

Is it preferable to never interpret dreams?

You cannot interpret dreams with elements from the waking state. Very often what we call dreams are made up of residues not fully lived in the waking state. But not all dreams are composed of residues. There are some elements which arise which have a very great significance. But you must live with them, not interpret them, because all interpretation is only approximate, so really live with them.

Can you speak to us about the fact that we take form in a body?

The body is a vehicle with which you should not identify. Discover the capacities of this vehicle in the moment itself, but don't identify with it. If you do, it leads to servitude.

Can intellectual understanding bring one to a letting-go of the mind or does all intellectual understanding keep one in mental bondage? Can it help to explain things?

One must go with thought to the end of all that is thinkable; and one will see, at a certain point, that thought, the mental, has its limits, that it can't understand what is beyond it, that everything it understands is in the subject-object relationship. When one really discovers that love, peace, joy, happiness cannot be thought, then thought will find its end and come to a stop. Then there is only being.

Thought can point to what is beyond it, but it can never comprehend it. Real understanding dissolves in silence.

Can I ask the question another way? Can psychology lead us to the threshold of knowing?

Psychology believes in the existence of the person and can dress the person in many, many ways. It can even appease, quiet, the person. It can also terrify the person as it often does. Nevertheless, it all turns around a more or less subtle person. But then if there wasn't a person for psychology, psychology would have no existence and a lot of people would have to look for other ways to earn a living, perhaps less successful ways.

Don't you think your approach also terrifies the person?

I would say, first find the person. I won't even say it doesn't exist, but find it. You haven't really looked for a long time. It is still only a belief, and as I am sure you will never find it, you will certainly, if you look hard enough, abandon the search.

252

T HE SILENCE WE SPEAK OF is beyond noise and quiet. When you speak of silence, you think of noise. But in the silence of which we speak any reference to quiet or noise is cancelled. It is a silence beyond all complementarity. And you live this silence in identity, not in duality but in oneness. When thought is completely absorbed in you, as happens from time to time, when it is completely exhausted, when there is nothing concrete left in thinking, then you live this silence, you are attuned to it. It cannot be objectified or experienced. It is not a state one enters and leaves. It is the light, the presence, the background of all expression, of all appearing and disappearing. There are many moments in the day when this silence is there, free from all activity. But as you are so accustomed to living in a subject-object relationship, you take this silence for an absence, an absence of something, an absence of activity. But this absence is the real presence.

Is this silence a vacuity?

A vacuity means vacant, absence of object. When there is absence of objects, there is plenitude. Fullness. Silence.

Silence is also manifest in movement.

Movement refers to silence. Everything refers to silence. It is only through this reference to silence that things are true; otherwise, they are false, abstract.

Who were the saints, like St. Francis of Assisi and Meister Eckhart?

Francis of Assisi had integrated knowingly the silence, lived in silence. He actualized the silence and we too are also this silence. But we are silence waiting to be actualized, we are potentially the silence. That is the only difference, to live in potentiality or actuality.

How can one at the same time cultivate the depths of body-feeling, and fan the flames in ourselves for the ultimate?

In this ultimate desire, our body knows its right place. It belongs to the totality. This ultimate desire is not a fixation, it is an expansion. We can feel it bodily. The person, the "me," is a fixation, a contraction. The desire for the ultimate leads us already into expansion, relaxation. Then, in a certain way, everything we do, everything we think is carried by this organic feeling of gentleness, vacuity, expansion.

Real communication is in silence where there is plurality. The personality belongs to individuality, singularity, but what we are functionally belongs to plurality. We are all the same, the same essence. In this silence there is at the same time communication and non-communication.

All our activities always refer to this background, this silence. All expressions of beauty, of life, refer to this silence.

Does there exist a silence of the body?

The body only has reality in silence. It has no reality in itself. It depends constantly on consciousness-silence. There is no reality outside of consciousness-silence. The body awakes in the morning *in* silence. Consciousness is. The body wakes up and with it the world. There is no world before the body wakes up. The world is only our corporeality, our five senses and the sixth sense, conception. There must be a body to perceive and conceive.

If the body functions mechanically, what is the place of consciousness?

It is consciousness which harmonizes the body, which harmonizes movement.

Would you define more precisely the word "harmonize," in this particular case?

To be harmonized means free from all conflict, free from all constraint, free from all antagonism. Something becomes harmonious when it refers to silence. All works of art, of poetry, painting, sculpture and architecture point to this silence. Every word points to the silence, to consciousness. We don't live words fully, a word points towards something. When one pronounces a word there is emotion, sensation. A word is not simply an abstract representation. There are words which do not stimulate great emotions in us, for example, chair, station or train. But when we say "light," when an actor pronounces "light" on the stage, it's not merely the light on his night-table or desk. It is the clarity, the light of God, truth, wisdom. All these are contained in the word "light." One must meditate on the word.

You spoke of the light of God. What is God?

When you say "god" it's a concept. But when you want to really live it, you can only live it in your absence. When one believes that the world was created, it is certain it was pronounced. When you really pronounce a word, you create an object.

Excuse me, is "pronounce" more subtle than "create"?

Pronunciation and creation are simultaneous.

Monsieur, please, yesterday you spoke about two types of thought, thought which comes from silence and thought which comes from memory. I am confused about the thought that comes from memory, because this thought

255

can provoke a self-judgment which I often confuse with the discrimination that comes from silence and permits me to really see a situation. How can I know the difference between thought which comes from silent discrimination and allows me a global vision, and thought which brings a certain form of judgment?

Scientific thought comes from thought. Thinking begins with a thought. But when one knows that the origin of thought is found in silence, then very often one combines discriminative, logical thinking with intuitive thought as, for example, in the artist. The artist at the same time utilizes his intuition and realizes his intuition in space and time with practical, rational thought.

When thought starts from thought, it is intentional. Such thought is led by the "me," by the person. It stays in a vicious circle. It is memory. It has not much extension. It is limited, not creative. But to come back to your question, bring back immediately the results of your thought to the one who knows thought. In other words, bring back what is seen to the seeing, what is heard to the hearing. At that moment, when you bring back what is heard to hearing, and what is seen to seeing, you sanctify the thought and you sanctify the situation.

I have a lot of difficulty understanding the tolerance of physical pain and the acceptance of that pain. Does acceptance come in the unification of the body, listening and exploration and the respect of the possibilities of the body?

One must accept pain not passively but actively. This means that when you accept the pain, it refers to the accepting itself, accepting in silence. Accepting is opening, receiving, welcoming, letting be with a view to knowing it. It is not a moral acceptance but a functional acceptance with a view to know something. The thing that you accept, it speaks, it offers its secret, it dissolves, it liberates itself. When you accept something, that thing becomes free, free in your acceptance. Our real nature is nothing other than accepting, that is, opening. You can never affirm acceptance and openness. The moment you affirm them, you objectify them. Acceptance is not an object, openness is not an object. In acceptance one must participate with the body, emotions. See how totally free you feel in this acceptance. We speak very much about emotions, feelings, perceptions; but when you accept a situation you are completely detached from it. This doesn't mean indifference, but seeing the situation very clearly.

The acceptance you are speaking about, is that volitional or natural?

When you find yourself knowingly in your real nature, the "I Am," all that solicits you in life is accepted. It is in the acceptance of a situation that there is a solution. There is no situation without a solution. In the essence of its composition is the solution. The solution is always instantaneous, abrupt. It does not pass through the discriminative mind where there is comparison and evaluation. In other words, a situation must be seen spontaneously in its totality, not through a mental division. To see a situation globally means seeing it without choice or selection, which comes from the "me," the individual point of view.

We are not accustomed to seeing the situations of our life in their globality, in an impersonal way. We know situations only in reference to our person. And any choice made from the stance of the person brings suffering, that is certain. We should see clearly what the person is, a collection of experiences with which we have identified.

This sensation of liberty in acceptance arises directly in the self? It is no longer enmeshed in the conditioning and conflicts of the ego?

Absolutely. Acceptance is an expression of our real nature. Acceptance is not an object. It is this acceptance that immediately frees what we accept. It frees us totally from conflicts. But it is not a concept, not a thought. It means that all that is perceived and conceived is accepted. Acceptance is not a thought, it is felt. So explore the sensation. Go with it to understand it. It is important to see how certain words release in us certain emotions and sensations; for example, this word "acceptance." When you understand really well the word acceptance, the accent is not on what we accept, it is placed completely on the accepting itself. And in this comprehension of the word acceptance, when you feel it really, there is a total letting-go. Welcome is even a better word than accept.

Is this acceptance which comes from silence detached from all emotional feeling? Should we just live the silence?

We are right to live this silence when we have discovered the limits of thought, when we have seen that it cannot be thought, that it does not come into the realm of thought. Then there is a complete letting-go.

Is there a reason for the forgetting of the self?

Your question is an asking for security for the "me."

Why?

If you live the absence of the why, the how, and the when very intensely, you will have the answer.

I think the important thing is to realize that the seeker is what he is seeking; the seeker is the found. You can never find the seeker. He is. All that you can find is an object. The seeker is the ultimate subject, what you are in your totality. When you have once understood that the seeker is the found, there is a total letting-go. All that we are looking for is objective—thoughts, representations—but what we are is unthinkable. So don't go into the frame of thinking. When you don't go in, there is an abandonment of thinking. The pulsations which create thought are at rest.

At that moment we need some manifestations of the silent teaching. Can it be manifested by gestures or looks?

I would say it is by sound or vibration. When a chord sounds, all other chords resonate. This is how the transmission occurs.

One must have the spark. It doesn't have anything to do with memory. Nevertheless you can knowingly refer to it. You will have it from time to time until there is a total establishing. It is not an emotivity but an emotion. Sometimes we confuse emotivity, which is a reaction, with emotion, which comes from beauty itself. One must live with this emotion.

Sometimes we feel harmony during the day, for example, in nature, and there is an emotion.

Then there is no thought.

But even though it is harmonious, there is still a subject-object relationship.

Yes, but before you objectify it, before you feel it in your body-mind, there is a moment of identity. It is enough that you know you can only live it in identity, not in duality. You know very well the moment you objectify harmony; when you say, "I am happy, I am content, I am integrated in the universe, I am the whole." All these are very grand feelings but nevertheless they are things perceived. So you must never objectify a perception. Never say, "I am happy." (laughter)

So it's the words, the formulation, that creates the separation?

Absolutely. It is absolute non-dual beauty which creates things in space-time, in three dimensions. It is a bad habit, a reflex, to objectify one's state of happiness.

I understand your formulation, "the seeker is the sought," but I don't quite understand "the seeker is the found." Do you mean the seeker is he who must be found?

The seeker *is* the found.

But I don't understand the present tense, the simultaneity.

The seeker is the sought.

That I understand, but the sought is very different from the found.

The seeker is the sought and the seeker is the seeker. (laughter)

259

Once sought, when one seeks, there is the found. You look to find and what do you want to find? Your plenitude! So you can only look objectively. When you have really understood this, then you awake in the subject, in the seeker.

So when there is comprehension there is the found?

There you are! It is important to understand this, that the seeker is the sought, because only then can you understand that all systems, techniques to reach something, to achieve, can only lead to an object.

It was the difference between the two formulations which . . .

Yes. One doesn't see it easily . . . (laughter)

So it is acceptance, the letting-go of our personality which allows the intuition?

Absolutely. And this subject, this acceptance, this opening is only welcoming. One cannot objectify it. It is an original perception. I think apperception may be more correct. It is a non-state which apperceives itself by itself. It has no need of an agent, an intermediary. One has it sometimes when one has understood something and there is only a representation; and this geometrical, logical, mathematical representation at a certain moment dissolves in a state that is no longer a state. One has the impression that all the formulations, all the energy that is still in the right brain is reabsorbed in the totality of energy, in the heart. In the end, something is perfectly understood when it has completely dissolved in the heart. Then there is no one who understands and nothing is understood. There is only being the understanding.

If the realization of the self is beyond the mental, what is the point of these dialogues and all the books?

They are a pretext, a pretext for coming together and to be here in joy without asking. This is quite rare!

What is pain? When one looks at it one sees tension, a lack of well-being. But it is very difficult to say what it is exactly.

Suffering, pain, is, above all, a perception. First there is a perception and afterwards the conception. That means you perceive and afterwards you analyze and formulate. The conception takes you away from what is real—the perception, the sensation, which you discover in your body. You must accept this sensation, but you will soon see how you resist it. You don't resist thoughts but you resist the sensation. You compensate, looking by every means in your repertoire, to superimpose on the actual sensation another sensation. In other words, you want to escape from the painful perception. So don't look for other elements, just accept the sensation without looking to compensate or escape. But we are not accustomed to seeing things like that, so you must learn to see things without defense, resistance, and judgment. This attention is acceptance. Then there is no more fuel for the sensation. The sensation is a reaction, a contraction; and as, in this attention, in acceptance, there is no room for a "me" which holds onto the perception, it can become free and unveil itself. To reveal itself fully takes some time, but there is every guarantee that it will dissolve in your attention.

But we must see clearly how we construct situations, how we function.

But why then do animals which don't judge or analyze or have an ego so obviously suffer?

It is a great art to look at something, to look the way an innocent child looks. See only that you don't look. We cannot say "I want to look" because we are the looking. We can only see how we don't look, how we interpret. Then we will find one moment when we are outside the process. It is a moment out of time and space. It is this moment which leads the transformation, the rectification. It erases the mistake. Only seeing things clearly can bring transformation. We can only see the false. We can never see the true because we are the true.

261

W

HAT CAUSES A CHILD TO CHOOSE ITS PARENTS?

When one has a child in one's arms, one must also be silent. When the child comes from the womb of the mother, it struggles to appropriate the world. The environment plays a big role in the child's constructing of its world. Your feelings and thoughts are also food for the child.

Regarding the body-work, is it good for children to do it?

I would say yes, but it depends on the age. One must understand the principle of the work and then adapt, simplify it. There are poses which are archetypes, but there are many poses which prepare the archetypes, prepare *the* pose.

Can children work with the sensation?

Absolutely. The child must be interested in the movement so his attention is present. At the beginning don't do it for very long. But it's very good.

Would you talk about consciousness in the innocent child?

Until the age of five or six the child uses mostly the right intuitive brain. There the child is present, not anticipating, not living in the

263

becoming process. When there is no intention, no intervention, there is purity of attention.

The cause of conflict in our life is, above all, anticipation to become. We live in psychological memory, past and future. Most people are very rarely present. Innocence refers above all to the absence of intention. As long as we think we are a personal entity there is intention. Because the entity can only live in a situation and as situations are very quickly exhausted, the entity lives in security, constantly looking to maintain itself. When there is intention there is the I-concept; in the absence of the concept "I" there is no intention. Life is in the present. Everything flows from the present.

When you observe a young child, you see the presence in his way of playing and looking, the innocence of his looking.

What is nostalgia?

It is an emotion, an emotion which comes directly from what you fore-feel, from your real nature. The adorer lives in what he adores. When he follows completely the current of his adoration, automatically he finds himself in the adored and then there is neither adored nor adorer. There is no longer duality. At that moment nostalgia dies completely. You must try to understand well this emotion, otherwise it could become a poison. Nostalgia which does not dissolve is a poison, a parasite.

You said once that the family is a poison, so I am asking how we choose our birth?

On the deepest level no one chooses his birth and on another level I would say one chooses one's mother and father. In choosing that particular father and mother, one finds some expansion, some maturity. So the father and mother have a big responsibility because the child is waiting for them. Then the family—that is another problem, the emotivities, old people, those who don't feel at home in themselves—it is a kind of nest one finds oneself in, it is also a poison. Freud called it "the smell of the nest." No, you must not only dream of this autonomy. It must not remain wishful thinking.

When there is love, the problem of affectivity no longer plays a role. Love is affection, affectivity belongs to the person. In love one is free, in affectivity people are stuck together. You must make the distinction, feel it clearly.

When one loses affectivity one finds oneself in autonomy. What allows this autonomy to remain indefinitely?

First have the fore-feeling of the autonomy. This fore-feeling comes from understanding. Understanding brings out the fore-feeling of truth. When you live this fore-feeling, one day you will find constant autonomy where you are no longer identified with what you are not, when you are really established in what you are fundamentally. Freedom is only to be free from oneself, the oneself one is not. It is important to remember every day what we are fundamentally—the "I" which has no qualities, the pronoun "I" which cannot be thought. It is an insight, an instantaneous feeling of being. So if you want a practice, there is the practice. As you see, there is nothing to practice, but if you want to call this "remembering" a practice, do so!

Can a doctor be the doctor for his parents if there is a serious illness?

He is a doctor and must heal. If the patient is a nephew or parent, that has nothing to do with it. There is a professional relationship. If he suffers with his patient, identifies with the patient, he cannot be a doctor. It is only in the non-identification that he can heal, because he is no longer an accomplice to the suffering. He may suffer as a son or daughter if the parent is ill but not as a doctor.

A real doctor can see more or less immediately where the illness arises, but he questions his patient as if he didn't know: "What do you feel? Hot? Cold? When?" He asks a lot of questions because he knows that the patient, in order to answer the questions, must look at his illness objectively, and in this there is some distance from the illness. It is this distancing which is the beginning of healing. So the doctor first helps his patient to distance himself from the disease. It is very magical, very profound. If a doctor doesn't understand this magic, he'd be better peeling potatoes.

This calls for acceptance. But one must love oneself before one can love others.

When I say one must love oneself before one can love others, I don't mean one must love one's personality. It means to discover love in oneself. When one has detected love in oneself one can see it in others. This is the highest role of the doctor. In his real role, he is a priest.

It is your presence above all which heals. That you call upon your science is an extension. But before everything, the patient must trust you. Then he is open, he accepts, abdicates. He knows that you take him in charge. The doctor prepares his patient to be a patient. At first the patient refuses the illness; refuses it, finds it unjust, says god is unjust, he does not deserve it, and so on.

There must not be any fixed relationship. In the non-relationship, the relationship appears. Take note how there was healing when you functioned in this way.

When you love someone, you are not an accomplice. But when you have a relationship with the other person's illness you feed it, you don't help it. Often sympathy is an accomplice with the one who is in pain. It is only in this non-relation that you can be a positive element.

From the highest view an illness reveals the one who knows it. The one who knows it is not ill, otherwise how could he know the illness? So illness is a pointer to ourselves. Illness points, leads to acceptance and this acceptance is our real nature. It is not an object but the total absence of all objectivity. Welcoming may be a better word. Welcome the perception, the illness.

I have difficulty in answering people who ask who you are and what role you play?

I have no role. I listen to the question in silence and the answer comes out of silence. So where is the questioner and where is the one who answers? They don't exist.

One must live with the answer and actually there are many occasions when I cannot answer with words. Silence is enough.

What is understanding?

The initial understanding is to understand what you fundamentally are not, that is, what you are only in extension, what has no reality in itself. Your body, your thoughts are only an extension of yourself. Your body only has a reality in consciousness. So see in you what is real and what is not real. All that is perceived has no reality in itself. It depends on a perceiver. The one who knows the body cannot be known. What is accepted can be known. He who accepts cannot be known. So be the accepting.

Thank you for coming.

For further information regarding Jean Klein and his schedule of talks and seminars in the United States and Europe, write to the Jean Klein Foundation, P.O. Box 941, Larkspur, CA 94977.

Those interested in Jean Klein's teachings may also wish to subscribe to the journal *LISTENING*, published twice a year. For subscription rates, write to the Jean Klein Foundation, P.O. Box 2111, Santa Barbara, CA 93102.

The mind sees from
· its conditioning -
truth is never found
· · there.
· · Listen for truth -

~Nothing new~